Love Virus

Jacci Turner

TREE HOUSE PRESS

Also by Jacci Turner

Find them all at www.jacciturner.com

Books for adults:

The Retreat

Tumbled People: Deconstructing and Reconstructing Your Faith

Books for Teens:

The Birthright Series: The Cage, The Bar, and The Lamb

Snapped

Cracker

Tree Singer

Middle Grade books for children aged eight and up:

The Finding Home Series: Bending Willow, Stretch-ing Willow, Finding Willow, Willow's Ride, and Willow's Roundup
  Shipwrecked

Dedication

To those who lost friends and family during the pandemic. I mourn with you.

CHAPTER ONE

Ashley

November 2019

Ashley was ready; she'd made up her mind. Thirty-five was too young to be tied to a man she didn't love, a man who frequently scared her, and had begun to disgust her. She sat on the small loveseat she'd bought with so much hope two years ago. He was charming then, handsome, and thoroughly able to hide the fact that he was a raging alcoholic. She should have known better; she met him at a bar.

Pepper and Westly, her rescue dogs, paced the small living room. They could tell she was nervous. Adopting the dogs had been the best choice she'd ever made.

She brought them with her from San Francisco. They were her friends and her support system. Mark hated them, of course. She'd begun to suspect that he left them outside all day when she was working out of town.

She took a deep breath and opened her front door. She shivered as the chill November air hit her. The dogs cavorted at her ankles, unsure if they were going outside. They stepped out onto the porch and sniffed. She lifted the suitcases and boxes full of Mark's things she had packed up and carried them out onto the small porch. She called the dogs in and shut the door. Now to wait.

This was the third night in a row Mark had not come home after work, it was already nine o'clock. The last two nights he'd come home smelling of whiskey and barked at her when she asked why he was late. This would stop . . . tonight. All they did was fight anymore. And her friends from work were sick of hearing about it. She finally got tired of hearing herself complain too. It was time for action.

Headlights swept by her front window as the car parked unevenly in front of the condo. She stood back from the front door, almost in the kitchen, breathing fast, her heart hammering. Her dogs stood on either side of her like sentinels. She heard Mark stumble up the steps, then stop. He must have noticed the boxes.

The door flew open as he charged in, his brown eyes blazing and his tie askew. "What's this?" he slurred, rage distorting his handsome face.

"Mark," she started, her voice squeaking. She took a breath and started again. "I want you out of my house."

"*Your* house? It's just as much mine as it is yours. *You* leave if you're unhappy. I'm sick of seeing your face, anyway. You used to be fun, now you're just a bitch."

He knew she hated when he called her that but she had coached herself not to rise to his bait. "All we do is fight and all you do is drink. You know it's my place. I need you to leave."

He came toward her, his face flushed, his eyes bulging.

Her heart was in her throat. Would he hit her? He never had, not with his fists anyway, just his words.

He stepped closer, but still out of striking distance. His hands were fisted. She started talking fast. "Look, I left San Francisco to be with you, and we found this place together. I'm not moving back there and I'm not moving out of the condo. I love it here."

He slowed and stood, swaying as if trying to process what she was saying, so she kept talking. "I love my job and my life in Reno, and I love my home."

"It's my house too."

"Mark." She tried to keep emotion out of her voice, hoping it might calm him. "You know it's my name on the contract, because of your bad credit."

"I helped pay the bills. and buy the furniture. I'm not leaving."

This wasn't true, she'd bought most of the furniture too, except the things he'd brought with him into the relationship, and most of those were old. She'd replaced them over time.

As he advanced toward her she stood her ground and held up her phone. "I've got 911 on speed dial. You need to leave, right now."

He took another step, his face purple with rage, but stumbled backward as her dogs jumped in front of her, barking and snarling. "I hate those fuckin' dogs of yours. You always liked them better than me."

Pepper's hackles were up and Westly crouched, moving slowly toward Mark, who backed toward the door. She had never seen them act this way.

"I'll be back, bitch. You haven't seen the last of me." He left then, slamming the door.

Pepper and Westly had never warmed up to Mark. She should have paid more attention to them in the first place. As soon as he was out the door, she dashed over and locked it, adding the chain latch. That wouldn't hold if he didn't want it to. She would change the locks first thing in the morning. She collapsed on the couch, her dogs on top of her, and buried her head in their fur. "Shittttt,' she sighed, shaking.

Would he really come back? Hot tears coursed down her cheeks, wetting Pepper's coat. She tried to slow her breathing.

Scraping and cursing came from the porch. She pushed the dogs off and stood to the side of the loveseat to peek out the window. Mark was loading his things into his Mustang, practically throwing them, kicking them when they dropped, having a full-on temper tantrum. She clutched her phone in her hand, ready to call 911 if he came back to the door. Once he'd finished loading, he looked up at the window, saw her peeking out, and used both hands to flip her off. He got into his car and screeched out onto the road. "Lord help anyone who gets in his way."

She closed the curtains and dragged the loveseat over in front of the door. If he came back, it might give her time to call the police. Then she flopped back on it and reached for the wine glass and the bottle of Merlot she'd placed on the coffee table earlier—liquid courage. She'd told herself she could not open it unless she'd kicked Mark out. She had done it!

She poured herself a glass with trembling hands, spilling a bit on the coffee table. It was done. She had finally taken control of her life and kicked the shithead out. Despite the fear and adrenaline coursing through her body, a small light of hope warmed her torso along with the wine. She'd made the right choice. This was the first step to getting her life back. She would sleep right here tonight, if she would sleep at all. She wanted to be ready in case he came back. But she would not let him in; this was her place now.

Her mind flew back to when they met. She was in nursing school in San Francisco, he, a traveling pharmaceutical rep who visited the doctor's office where she served as an intern. One night after work she and two friends had stopped at a bar for a glass of wine, and she saw him. He was gorgeous, with dark eyes and golden-brown skin. It was his easy manner and confidence that had won her over. He wanted her to drop out of school and move to Reno with him right away. Thankfully, she made him wait until graduation.

Even so, their relationship had moved too fast. She knew that now. She moved out of her apartment as soon as she graduated and headed east. Mark suggested they move in together right away but his credit was lousy, so he didn't qualify for a bigger place. That should have been a red flag. She knew pharmaceutical reps made a lot of money. Why was he living in a studio apartment? Why did his credit score suck?

She moved in with him. It felt very cozy even though the dogs were in the way. She worked twelve-hour days at the hospital, so they were seldom home at the same time. Soon she had saved enough to buy this place. Then she found an even better job although it involved a lot of travel. Maybe that's why it took her so long to figure out who Mark really was. Or was it just denial?

It was lust, pure and simple . . . lust had clouded her mind. He was charming, and a passionate lover. He was also an alcoholic, a gambler, and she suspected he saw other women on the side. She took a shaky breath, glad to be rid of him at last. She had done it.

CHAPTER TWO

Maya

November 3, 2019

Senior English Reflection Paper.

Writing Prompt: Tell us about your worst day as if it just happened.

On Day-One of my senior year of high school, I ended up in the dean's office. This was not how I wanted to start at a new school.

I am, I mean, I *was* excited about starting my senior year at Sierra High. This year was going to be great! Next June I'll turn seventeen and Dad will let me get my license. This year I hope to have a boyfriend. Mom, Dad, and I moved to Reno, Nevada this summer for

Mom's job. She is a great pediatrician already, I can tell by the stories she tells us over dinner. She loves her patients and they love her.

Anyway, this is what happened.

It's my first day of school. I walk into the cafeteria, and the usual smell of fries and pizza hits my nose. I can tell you that all cafeterias smell the same, no matter what part of the country you're in. I've moved a lot. It's loud too, the sound bounces off the walls.

Anyway, I walk into the cafeteria and see Karly and Keesha standing by a table, two of the newly minted friends I met at a summer camp for girls interested in science and math. Yep, I'm that person, uber-smart and unashamed of it, a lot like my mom. I lived here before, when Mom was at the university getting her pre-med, but I was just a little kid, so I really don't have any friends from before. I was glad to meet these girls this summer. I feel pretty good about my first-day look: skinny ripped jeans and a sleeveless white top. I straightened my black hair, so it's sleek. I fight my way through the crowd in the caf to get to Karly and Keesha. "Heyyy," I say. It's our usual greeting, a drawn-out Hey.

"Heyyy," Keesha echoes, her soft curls looking especially on point today. "Did you hear Jonell is looking for you?"

Jonell is another girl I met this summer at STEM camp, and when she came over to my house for a sleepover this summer, she turned the whole thing into a big drama, saying one of the girls has been flirting with her boyfriend. She stomped out halfway through the night, leaving all of her stuff at my house, which is now sitting in my closet waiting for her to come to get it. I wasn't planning to hang out with her this year. I don't like drama. "What does she want?"

"Don't know." Keesha shrugs.

"I heard she wants her stuff back." Karly tosses her blonde hair off her shoulder and pops her ever-present gum.

"Her stuff?"

"The stuff she left at your house when she left in the middle of the party."

"Oh. She could come get it anytime. It's been sitting in my room all summer." The next thing I know, I see Karly's eyes grow round and I'm being swung around by my arm. I'm nose-to-nose with Jonell, whose face is as red as her hair, and I don't think she brushed her teeth this morning.

"Ow, that hurts." I rub my bare arm. And she pushes me. "Whoa, what was that for?" I barely keep my balance. Is she joking?

"You stole my stuff." She pushes me again.

"Stop it. Your stuff is sitting in my room where you left it..." and her fist is in my face before I can finish the sentence. My nose explodes in pain and I fall on the hard cafeteria floor. My mind is a blur of thoughts.

What's happening?

Why is she doing this?

Movies lie to us. One punch to the face and no one is jumping right up for more.

And the last thought is: *"Ewe,* somebody get me off this gross floor." Dirt and greasy fries and an army of shoes around me. *This is the first day of school, people, this floor should be spotless.*

Jonell bends over me and keeps hitting me on my head. I turn to try to grab her hands, but she hits my face and I lash out at her, trying to keep her off me.

"Help me," I scream. I can see my friends through the fists, standing by and watching like zombies. Other kids have their phones out. *Are you freakin' kidding me? They're* filming *this?*

Then a teacher comes up and I think, *Finally, some help.* The teacher pulls Jonell off me, then drags me off the floor with her other hand and pulls us both through the cafeteria and down the hall to the office. I don't know this teacher, but she seems really pissed and quite strong. Blood is flowing out of my nose during my walk of shame. My crisp white top is now dirty and bloody. I wipe the blood with my hands, trying not to cry.

The office lady hands me a box of tissues, concern on her face. The unnamed teacher lowers me into a chair and puts Jonell in a seat as far from me as she can. I sneak a glance at Jonell, who is glaring at me. At *me,* like *I've* done something wrong. She has a few scratches on her face. The teacher heads up to a door marked Dean's Office and knocks.

A muffled "Enter" comes from the other side of the door and she pushes in.

We sit there for what seems like hours but is probably only minutes. I have never been in trouble at school before. I'm a good kid with great grades and this is the weirdest thing that has ever happened to me. Of course, nobody here knows that. It's my first day. Not the best way to make a good impression.

Finally, the unnamed teacher leaves the dean's office fast, like she's got somewhere to be, and gives us a *You behave!* glare as she exits. We sit there for another twenty minutes. The office lady goes back to her typing but sneaks furtive looks at us as if we might be plotting to burn down the school.

Finally, a man I assume is the dean, who looks like an athlete gone to seed: tall, broad-shouldered, with a paunch over his belt, invites me into his office and gestures at a chair for me to sit in. His room has the spicy smell of some kind of aftershave. He takes his place behind a large wooden desk and glances at a piece of paper. "Miss Hunter, is it? . . . Maya?" He looks at me over his glasses. I wonder how he figured out who I am.

"Yes." My voice shakes as I speak around the tissue. Like I said, I have NEVER been in an office like this. My only reference point is from movies, and that never goes well for the kids involved. I look beyond him at the "Live your best life NOW" poster tacked crookedly on the wall over his shoulder and have to squelch a desire to laugh. That's me all right, living my best life.

"Tell me what happened." The dean speaks in a monotone like he's said this a million times.

It's the first day of school and yet he looks as bored as I am terrified. "I was just standing in the cafeteria with my friends, and Jonell walked up and started punching me."

He tilts his head. I can tell he doesn't believe me. "Surely, you must have done something to upset her?"

"No, I really didn't. I was just standing there. You can ask my friends."

There is a knock at the door, and the dean says, "Come in."

In walks my father. I guess Mom is working and I'm not sure I'm disappointed; Mom can be a bit much. And Dad's a big guy; he works construction, and looks like it. There's no paunch hanging over *his* belt. He takes one look at me and gets right up to the dean's desk. "What happened to my daughter?"

The dean doesn't budge. In the same flat voice, he says, "Please take a seat, Mr. Hunter."

My dad stands there for a minute. I can tell he wants to throttle the dean. Eventually, he sits next to me but leans forward, he's in Papa Bear-mode and turns to me with a worried look, which makes my shoulders relax. He'll take care of this. He'll make it better.

Dad looks at me, his forehead creased. "What happened, pumpkin?"

That does it. I start to cry. First, out of embarrassment because he called me 'Pumpkin' in front of the dean, and second, because he called me *Pumpkin*, and I feel five years old. And now, of course, I'm ugly-crying and hiccupping, and can't even talk right. "Jonell...*hic*...hit...*hic*...me," is the best I can do.

"It seems," interrupts the dean, "that your daughter was in a fight."

"My daughter doesn't fight," Dad insists. "Did you see that girl out there? She hardly has a mark on her. What I want to know is why she beat up my daughter, and what you're going to do about it."

"While I do hope to get to the bottom of this," the overly calm dean says, "we at Sierra High have a strict non-violence policy. I'm afraid Maya here has earned herself a three-day-suspension and will not be invited back onto campus until she has completed the district's three-day Anti-violence curriculum.

"WHAT?" Dad sounds as shocked as I feel. "But she didn't do anything. She's new here so you don't know her. She's a great student and has never been in trouble."

You tell him, Dad. I nod along like a bloody, snot-dripping bobblehead.

"You didn't do anything, did you, pumpkin?" He turns to me with a look that asks: *You didn't, did you?*

Again with the 'Pumpkin'? I cringe. "No." I widen my eyes at him. Of course I didn't. My voice sounds nasal as I shake my head, noticing that my neck hurts. I continue to hold a tissue to my nose. How is there this much blood in my head? My lap is full of used bloody tissues.

"I'm sorry," says the dean. "The teacher who brought the girls in arrived at the scene as both girls were engaged in a fight. Therefore, both must receive consequences." With that, he hands my dad a card and stands as if to dismiss us. "Here's the information you'll need to get Maya enrolled in the classes. She will need a parent to attend with her. She is welcome back as soon as the classes are finished."

And that was the worst thing that ever happened to me.

CHAPTER THREE

LaRue

November 2019

LaRue stepped out of her car which she'd parked by the Truckee River. The river runs right through the middle of Reno and is a gathering place during warm weather for kayakers, swimmers, and sunbathers, not to mention those down on their luck. November is still beautiful in Reno when they have a long fall. She loved her church, the 150-year-old Methodist church that she'd found late in life, but it didn't have any parking. Not that it mattered, at 75, the walk was good for her.

"You know, Walter, the doctor said the best thing for arthritis is walking, to keep the joints lubricated." She didn't say it out loud, of course, Walter had been dead ten years now and she didn't want people to think she was crazy. She was just used to talking to him.

She crossed the street and walked the three blocks up to the church, grateful for her comfy light cotton capris and arch-support sandals. A lot of people were out today, some even in the river, playing in the man-made rapids. It was hot out and there was still smoke in the air from the California fires. It had been like this all summer and the fall had not cooled off, but the smoke was lifting. Because Reno is in a valley, smoke from the forest fires settles in for months, sometimes so thick they caution people not to leave their homes. At least it wasn't that bad today.

She looked at the swimmers and marveled at their young, healthy bodies. She remembered how the riverfront was a dirty, neglected part of the city when she and Walter came to Reno 38 years ago. But now it looked quite nice. A light breeze ruffled her gray curls, and it felt fantastic. She smiled to herself. *If I got in that water, they'd need to call an emergency crew to pull me out.*

The trees were starting to turn, just a titch. Fall was her favorite time of year; it never lasted long enough for her. Often, just when the trees had turned beautiful reds and yellows, they'd have a hard frost, and the wind would come up and take all the leaves down. She hoped this year would be different.

She entered the church from the office entrance. Since the church was downtown, a lot of odd people wandered in, so there was always someone at the desk, behind a glass partition. Today it was Silvia, the new church secretary. "Hello, LaRue," Silvia called. "You here for the Loaves and Fishes?"

"Yep, heading there now." LaRue stopped at the entrance to let her eyes adjust to the darker room.

"'The girls' are already here. They'll be glad to see you. Fred called to say he couldn't come, has a cold."

"Oh dear, I'll add him to my prayer list. See you later, Silvia."

LaRue turned left to the hall that led to the kitchen and large gymnasium-type community room. The room had the musty smell of old buildings, mixed with coffee. That meant Jackie was here, she was the self-appointed coffee maker at the church.

"Howdy-hi, friends and neighbors," she called as she entered the room.

Betty and Jackie both poked their heads out of the open kitchen area and waved. These were her two closest friends. Seeing their faces always made her smile. She didn't mind living alone with her cat Hershey, but sometimes it was good to see her friends.

Jackie, a fit-looking woman with short spiky hair came out of the kitchen. "Do you want to work with us today, or go down with Donna and Bev? They're in the packing room with Gerald."

LaRue laughed. Jackie was all business and energy. "I'd like to stay with you two, of course."

"Good," said Jackie. "I'll put you on sandwiches."

Because the church was downtown, it had an active ministry to the poor. Every Tuesday they made fresh sandwiches to go with the food baskets for those in need. People would line up tomorrow morning for the food, and LaRue always felt good to help those less fortunate than herself.

Jackie handed her a plastic apron as she led her into the kitchen. Betty was there already, sitting on a stool with her portable oxygen tank on the floor beside her. She was the shortest of the three and almost as round as she was tall. "Uh-oh," said LaRue. "Are you having a 'bad-air' day?"

Betty chuckled. She had COPD and LaRue called the days she needed to be on oxygen bad-air days. "I'll be fine. It's just these stupid fall allergies. I hate it because it's so beautiful out, now that the smoke from the fires has mostly cleared out, but the rabbitbrush is in full bloom. Damned if I do and damned if I don't."

"Well, you rest. Jackie and I can whip these out in no time."

"Glad to," said Betty, sipping coffee. "Oh, there's coffee for you." She gestured to the fresh pot and LaRue stopped to help herself, adding cream and one Splenda. Her days of adding sugar were gone as it seemed to inflame her arthritis.

The kitchen was a long narrow room and Jackie pulled out a cardboard box full of bread, heading out of the kitchen into the common room. "I'll lay the bread out if you come next with the mayo and mustard. I've already washed the table. We've got ham and cheese today."

"Ham and cheese, what a treat," said LaRue. They got their food from the food bank and worked with whatever was donated that week. Ham and cheese was a rarity; usually it was peanut butter and jelly.

Before she could follow, Betty grabbed her wrist. "LaRue, did you hear Fred was out with a cold?"

"Yes, poor guy. Though I wonder if it's allergies."

"Well, I was thinking it would be nice if you took him some soup or something."

LaRue shook her head. Ever since she started attending this church her friends were always trying to matchmake her. "You're incorrigible," she teased. "I've told you a million times I'm not interested. I had a beautiful marriage to Walter and that is good enough for me. Just because you two," she looked out of the open kitchen at Jackie, who was listening intently, which confirmed LaRue's belief they'd dreamed up this scheme together, "found love late in life doesn't mean I need to." Both women were in second marriages after divorces. Betty had Dennis and Jackie had Cathy, and both were quite happy.

Jackie looked at Betty; both women shrugged. LaRue knew they'd keep trying. She didn't really mind. She opened the fridge to pull out industrial-sized jars of mayonnaise and mustard. She was just glad to have friends who cared about her.

She'd met Walter at Kansas State University, she, a wide-eyed freshman, and he, a tall, handsome junior. They'd fallen desperately in love and, against her parents' wishes, married. She dropped out to support him as he went from an Animal Science major to Vet School. She didn't mind; life with Walter was all she wanted . . . even after several miscarriages when they realized there would be no children. She'd poured herself into his veterinary practice and they had adopted a stream of abused and neglected pets. Those were her babies.

LaRue pulled on latex gloves and carefully spread mayonnaise across the slices of bread and added a bit of mustard. Whether mustard was a spice or a condiment had been one of the things she and Walter disagreed on. She saw it more as a spice, wanting only a little on a sandwich, he wanted it to equal the mayonnaise. She smiled at the memory.

Jackie followed after her with slices of cheese and ham. The repetitive motion allowed LaRue's mind to wander. When no children came they decided to move west, and ended up in Reno. Walter opened his own veterinary clinic where he spent the next 38 years, until cancer took him. She'd been by his side the whole time. Nope, she did not need another man, she'd had the best the universe had to offer already.

Chapter Four

Maya

January 1st, 2020

Well, it's a new year so I've decided to start a journal and cheat by using the paper I wrote for the Senior English class as my "prequel." We're on Christmas break and I'm enjoying my cozy new comforter as I sit on my bed. Let me just summarize: school got better.

My dad and I got through the anti-violence program fast, which is a huge relief. Then I had three days to be nervous about returning to school. Every time I walked into the anti-violence class, I felt like a convict.

Plus, I never saw Jonell in class, so I don't think she was punished at all.

My mom took Jonell's stuff and dropped it off on the porch of her house. Mom was spoiling for a fight. Not a physical one, but she can cut a person down to size with words faster than you can say uncle. Lucky for them, no one was home.

Mom is the reason I decided to write in a journal. Our relationship is complicated, and we fight a lot. She's fierce when she gets her back up. You should have seen her when she got home from work and heard the story about the consequences over the fight. I think she must have called every person on the school board to complain, and I had to beg her to drop it when she tried to get the dean fired. That's all I needed, more negative attention at my new school.

There was fallout at school, of course, from the videos, which went viral immediately. I couldn't walk down the hall without someone commenting about the fight, shadowboxing as I walked by, or saying, "Hey, it's Rocky," and laughing like it was the funniest thing ever.

I had always been able to blend in at my past schools, but not here. I was a hot topic from Day-One, and I hated it.

I tried to avoid Jonell and her friends. When I passed them in the hall, my stomach clenched and I thought I might vomit. Jonell glared at me like I was spoiled meat, and my heart raced. Would she jump me again? She didn't, just kept walking, glaring at me as I passed. It was awful and I shook for like an hour afterward.

Plus, those two girls I'd met at camp—Karly and Keesha. I thought they were my friends but they dropped me like a used tissue. Shannon was there for me, though. She's another friend I made at STEM camp. She was in the library during the fight and continues to be my friend. I'm grateful for that, cause we have a lot of the same advanced placement classes, so I usually have someone to sit by.

In August, when I came back to school, my nose and eyes were still pretty colorful and swollen. The doctor said my nose was broken and to wait two weeks to see if it healed funny. If it did, they'd be glad to rc-break it. *Yikes!* So far, it looks like it healed straight, and Mom's been keeping an eye on it. I walked into

Chemistry feeling like everyone was staring, and the teacher sent me to sit by a boy named Sam, my new lab partner. He took one look at me and said, "Love the look. Are you dressing to match your bruises?" I could tell by his smile he was teasing.

"Hey," I joked back. "It wasn't easy to find a shirt in this shade of purple and blue."

He grinned at me and we started measuring ingredients. That was that. Sam's pretty cute. His shoulders are broad from swimming, and he has these really expressive blue eyes. Anyway, Sam has treated me like I'm a normal person instead of a troublemaker. He began eating lunch with Shannon and me and some of her other friends. He's very sweet.

The last day before Christmas break, it's after lunch, and Sam is walking with me to our chemistry class. "Guess what?" he says.

"What?" Changing classes at Sierra High always makes me feel like I'm a salmon swimming upstream.

"I'm getting a car for my birthday . . . after Christmas."

"Cool!" I practically yell to be heard over the racket in the hallway.

"What kind?"

"It's an old Dodge. My brother is handing it down to me, but it's A CAR." We stop outside of our class to finish the conversation.

"Do you have a license?"

"Nope, I get to take the test during spring break though, and I was wondering if you'd like to go somewhere with me. Like a movie or something? Test out the new wheels."

My heart may have stopped beating right then and there. "Sure," I blurt out and wonder if it is meant to be like a date or just as friends.

"Cool." He smiles his cute smile which quirks up a bit on one side. "I can't wait." He heads into the classroom.

"Okay," I stammer, wondering if he can't wait because of me, or because of the car. Then he smiles at me over his shoulder and my heart thumps and suddenly I'm thinking about prom dresses and having my first boyfriend.

After that, the semester wasn't all bad. My classes are challenging, and Shannon, Sam, and I enjoy hanging out at lunch. Nothing big has happened between

Sam and me yet. Just some fun flirting. People seem to have forgotten about the fight and I'm glad about that. Other school dramas have taken their attention, I guess. Mostly, I'm just applying for colleges and trying to keep my grades up and trying to stay warm. Reno can be cold in the winter.

I want to go to med school and be a doctor like my mom, though maybe not a pediatrician. The stories she tells about work at dinner are tough. Sick and injured kids are hard to hear about.

Anyway, like I said, I decided to write a journal because I want to talk about Mom. Mom is this beautiful, fierce Italian. She is passionate about everything, especially me. I mean, I understand, she came here from Italy and had to learn the language and culture; it was tough. And as a woman in med school she didn't have it easy. No one expects female doctors to be stunning.

Mom felt terrible about moving me again this year, but to be honest, I didn't mind. We ping-ponged around a lot during her training to become a pediatrician. First, she did her four years of medical school in Reno. Then to Allentown, Pennsylvania for her residency. Then we moved to Grand Rapids, Michigan for three years for her general pediatrics. Dad said he would follow her anywhere as long as they landed back in Reno when she finished, because his brother, Todd and his wife Nancy, and their kids, my three cousins, live here. So that's what we did.

I love her, but she is on me ALL THE TIME.

"Are you studying?" . . . "Shouldn't you be studying?" . . . "Did you finish your studying?"

It's making me CRAZY!

I mean, we had a good Christmas and she bought me some nice clothes—she has great taste, and I keep getting taller—so it was fun to shop, but as soon as the day was over it was back to "Did you finish those applications?" I mean can't a girl even take some time off?

So, when Mom announced she was going to Italy to help her mom, my nonna, who is having a double hip replacement, I must say I was relieved. I go in to help her pack, thinking it will be the last time I see her for a while and it'll be nice to spend some time together. I sit on my parent's California King bed which smells of Mom's favorite perfume, while she lays her clothes out on the bed. She's going to be gone for a month or more, depending on how Nonna heals, so she has to make some decisions about what to take.

I feel like we've been fighting all semester, but I'm determined to send Mom off on a good note. "Mom, you know they have a washing machine, right?" I tease. She smiles and it lights up her whole face.

Score one for me.

"And what will you do while I'm gone?" She has stacked her tops and sweaters on the bed and is now rolling them into a ball to put into her suitcase. She's a world-class packer and says this trick keeps things from getting too wrinkled.

"Well," I think hard, I know what she wants me to say. "I'll study, of course. Send out the applications, and hang out with Shannon and Sam." I say the last part quickly hoping to sneak it by her.

She stops and looks up at me, her black eyes flashing. "I don't want you with that boy when I'm not here. I don't want anything to come between you and your studies."

Anger fills me. "Mom, I have to have friends. I'm a good student. You should be able to trust me by now."

Her hands move to her hips, and her accent gets thick when she is angry. "You are too young for boys." She shoves her black flats into the suitcase.

"I'm going to be seventeen. It's not my fault you made me skip a grade."

This is an old wound. I shouldn't have poked it. We have fought about it off and on since it happened. I didn't want to skip a grade, but she pushed the decision through. Why did I bring it up? Sometimes it's like I can't help myself. I just have to goad her. I wish I could resist the temptation, but I know just what to say to tick her off.

Then she starts yelling in Italian and gesturing wildly. I can only understand a few words, like "focused" and "sacrifice."

I jump to my feet. "Fine! I'll be a nun in a convent. Is that what you want?" I stomp out and slam the door behind me.

I feel bad now. Of course, we hugged and kissed at the airport. Mom doesn't hold a grudge. Her anger flares up and is gone, but why are moms so difficult? I just want a normal mom/daughter relationship like Lorelai and Rory on the Gilmore Girls. Is that too much to ask? Mom and I watched every episode. We are so like them, Mom was young when I was born, and we're both smart, and love to read and banter. But we fight way more than they do. Maybe writing about it will help me figure out how to get along with her.

CHAPTER FIVE

LaRue

January 2020

LaRue sat in her cozy recliner, her cat Hershey on her lap smelling of LaRue's rose scented perfume. Betty, and Jackie prepared to watch *The Crown* on TV. This was "their show," and LaRue loved their weekly girl's night gathering. Sometimes in the winter, when it was too icy to drive, they'd watch from their homes and talk together on the phone afterward. But tonight, the weather was clear.

Betty sat on the couch and Jackie came in from LaRue's kitchen with two bowls full of popcorn. LaRue loved that the girls were so comfortable in her home that they could help themselves to her kitchen. Jackie had brought kettle corn tonight. She handed LaRue a bowl and then took her place on the couch next to Betty.

"I just love Helena Bonham Carter as Princess Margaret, don't you?" asked Betty.

"Oh, she's my favorite," agreed Jackie. "I watched all the Harry Potters with my grands, and she was so good in those movies. Creepy."

LaRue laughed. She wished she had grandchildren, but she lived vicariously through her friends' stories. She had sort of adopted the little girl across the street. It was like having a surrogate granddaughter. "Do you think I'd like those Potter movies?"

"Well, I did," Jackie crunched on the kettle corn. "But then, I read all the books too. I try to keep up with the kids' interests so we have something to talk about. But I did enjoy them."

LaRue made a mental note to try and find the books on her next visit at the library. She loved to read and prided herself on reading a wide variety of things, though she was not fond of science fiction.

"If it's not a romance, I'm not interested," said Betty. Betty was Hallmark-movie all the way. Every Christmas she made the girls sit through several of those, although LaRue could have done without the predictable plots. "Don't you think Olivia Colman is doing a great job as the queen?"

"Oh yes," agreed LaRue. "I just wonder what the real queen thinks of this show. Do you think she watches it? *Ouch.*"

"What happened?" asked Jackie, looking startled.

"Hershey bit me . . . well, not *bit* me exactly; didn't break the skin. Darn cat tried to eat my popcorn," She pushed the cat off her lap. He scowled at her as he slunk away.

"I don't know what you see in that fat old cat," said Betty.

"Probably the same thing you see in that grouchy old dog of yours," said LaRue. "He still peeing on the carpet?"

"No, not since we got him on the diabetes medicine."

"What's the news from the 'orange menace'?" asked Jackie. "I didn't have time to read the paper this morning."

LaRue knew she was referring to their president. All three were avid members of the Reno Dems and spent a lot of time bemoaning the current administration. "Did you hear what he said about that new virus in China?"

"No. What?" asked Jackie.

"That it's just one person coming from China, and not to worry," said LaRue.

"That probably means we should worry," said Betty.

"You know my little Maya?" LaRue glanced out the window at the large Victorian across the street. Maya was the closest thing she had to a granddaughter, and her friends knew that.

"What?" asked Betty, concern etching her face.

"Her mom, Sophia, the Italian goddess I always talk about, went to Italy to care for her mother after hip replacements—both hips. I told her I'd keep an eye on Maya and Jonathan."

Jackie picked up the remote as it was almost time for their show. "Do you think it's safe to travel right now?"

LaRue glanced out of the window again. "That's what I was wondering."

"I'm sure she'll be fine. She's a doctor," said Betty.

LaRue couldn't help but worry. This virus was heating up. China was closed down . . . China! It was no time to travel. Little Maya, who wasn't so little, and her dad were scared. She could see it in their faces whenever they stopped by to check on her. Maya's dad, Johnathan, was like a big bear on the outside, but soft on the inside. She knew he worked hard for his family and adored his wife and daughter. If anything happened to Sophia, what would become of them? "I'm just worried."

'*Shhh.*" Jackie unmuted the TV. "It's time."

LaRue pulled her thoughts away from the family across the street. Not for the first time she wondered if people who had died had any sway in the physical world. "Walter, if you can, would you please help Sophia and her parents over in Italy be okay? Bring her home safely. I mean, . . . if you can." She didn't really believe he could change anything, but sometimes it made her feel better to ask. Gratitude. That's what she tried to practice when she was in a cycle of worry. She had a great life with Walter and, although it was devastating when he left her, she had a good life now.

She looked at her friends and felt a wave of contentment run through her. Who needed a man when she had friends to watch her show with, and an ornery old cat that she loved? Her life was full of political involvement, serving the poor, and sharing time with her friends. "I've done all right without you, haven't I, Walter?" She knew he would agree.

CHAPTER SIX

Ashley

January 2020

Ashley stood behind the Champion Health display at the National Conference of Health Workers. This room was set up for tabling, a practical space in a beautiful hotel. She felt smart and proud after successfully presenting her company's PowerPoint deck to a room full of doctors, hospital administrators, and other health professionals. She'd been able to answer all their questions after the presentation, and the thumbs-up from her boss afterward hadn't hurt at all.

Now she was in a conference room full of tables, like hers, each representing some health-related company.

It was a chance for people to talk to each company's representatives and get their questions answered.

The room filled with conference attendees as each of the last seminars finished for the day and folks mingled, holding their before-dinner drinks. It felt good to be done with her presentation; now she could relax.

A handsome man in a sharp black suit came up to the booth and smiled. "Hello, I'm John Chen." He reached out his hand and she shook it. When he smiled at her she felt a little flutter in her chest; he had amazing dimples.

"Ashley Matheson. Nice to meet you, John."

"I enjoyed your presentation. Can I get one of those free books you talked about?"

She grabbed a copy of the book off the table. She was proud of that too. She'd written most of it to explain how companies like Champion Health worked, helping hospitals and clinics get Medicare funding by showing improvement in their preventative health numbers. The company's design team had done a great job making the graphs and statistics attractive.

But she'd done the work of putting it together. "Here you go."

"I was interested in your new model for rural clinics. I work with some in Eastern Washington. I have a dinner meeting, but would you join me for a drink after dinner to discuss it more in depth?"

Ashley felt her face flush, was he hitting on her? This man was very attractive, and she hadn't been on a date since she kicked Mark out. Of course, getting untangled from Mark and their overlapping commitments had taken months. Why not have a little fun? "That would be lovely. Shall I meet you at the bar?" She glanced at his left hand to make sure there was no ring or tan line where a ring should be. She hated that people used conferences as an excuse to cheat on their spouses.

"Perfect. I'll see you then." He smiled, his dimples deepening, and turned to leave, turning around once more and waving the book at her with a silent "Thanks."

Ashley felt a thrill run down her spine. What should she wear? She needed to get out of this business suit before tonight. In her nervousness about the presentation she'd probably perspired, and now felt like a wilted flower. She was to staff the booth for another half-hour, until four-thirty. Dinner was at five-thirty, which would give her time to shower and change.

Happiness and excitement flooded her; it had been so long since she'd felt attractive. Of course, maybe he did just want to talk about rural clinics. Was he a doctor? He hadn't introduced himself that way. Maybe he was a humble doctor . . . that'd be a first. She'd been a nurse in a hospital for the first year after graduating, but only spent six months in patient care before realizing she didn't like it. Working for Champion Health allowed her to influence patient care in a much broader way. She was able to travel over the western states, training doctors and nurses in preventative care, and helping them improve their profits in the process. A win-win.

She spent the next half-hour daydreaming about Eastern Washington, although a few more people came up to ask for the free book. *That part of Washington is high desert, not that different from Reno, and it's a straight shot up Highway 395. What would a long-distance relationship be like?* At 4:30 she packed away the important things on the table, putting them into a box and sliding it under the table out of sight. It was time to go get ready.

Ashley headed to the bar of the hotel convention center, glad she'd packed the slinky emerald green wrap dress and her spiked heels. She felt sexy. Was it too much? Dinner had been fun, with some of the bigwigs from the company and basking in their praise; "...your excellent work makes us look good." Champion Health was a smaller company; most of the top brass part of the same family. She'd been glad they'd taken a risk on her and wanted to prove herself. Today, just one year later, she had. But she mostly pushed her food around her plate, nervous about meeting John. It had been four years since she'd been on a real date. *Were those four years wasted on Mark? And is this even a date?*

John sat at the bar, stirring a drink with his swivel stick. She appreciated the way his shirt tugged tight against his back muscles as she walked up. Gone was the suit, replaced by gray slacks and a button-up black linen shirt.

"Hello." She slid onto the barstool beside him and touched his arm. Various sports events blared from TV sets around the room. He turned from the one nearest him and gave her an appraising look.

"Wow," he said. "I thought you looked great before, but tonight you're killing it."

She laughed. A man had not complimented her since the early days of her relationship with Mark. Of course, *he'd* been charming too. The thought brought her back to reality. *I don't know this man,* she reminded herself. *Remember Mark.* He was now her cautionary tale. *You met him in a bar. But this is different, right?* She didn't meet John in a bar, she met him at a health convention. They just happened to be sitting in a bar. "What can I get you?" He held up his drink. "I'm having a Black Russian, it's a treat."

"Oh fun. I'll have a White Russian; they're even better."

He signaled to the female bartender and ordered for Ashley. "So, are you worn out after such a full day?"

"Not yet, but I'll definitely sleep well tonight. My part of this convention is over. How about you?"

"My presentation is tomorrow, then we all head home. Where do you live?"

"Reno." She took the drink the bartender set in front of her, stirring it a bit and taking a sip. Sweet liquid with a kick made its way to her stomach. "It was pretty cold when I left. Nice to be in Texas for a change."

"Cold in Walla Walla too. I needed thawing out."

"So, you work with some clinics there?"

"I run three in the region, actually. Do you ever come up to do training in my area?"

She grinned. He did not just work with them, he ran them. She took another sip; warmth filled her chest. "Yep, Walla Walla is definitely in my area." Not only might she have a date, but she could get three more clinics for her company. Her boss would be thrilled. "You'd have to sign with Champion, of course."

"Of course, but your presentation sold me on that today." He finished his drink. "Would you like another?

She'd only drunk half of her drink but nodded and took a large gulp. Her head felt good, happy, and relaxed. *Why am I feeling the alcohol already? Maybe because I've barely eaten today. First, preparing for my seminar I missed lunch, and then skimped on dinner out of nerves. Oh well, why not live a little? I'm celebrating, I did a good job and I just scored three new clients for my company.*

"Is Chen a Chinese name?" She tipped her first drink and drained the last of the sweet elixir, setting the glass down as the bartender replaced it with a new one. *I need to be careful. Slow down, Ashley.*

"Yes. I'm second-generation, but on my mom's side I'm mostly Scottish."

"Do you still have family in China? And are you concerned about that virus?"

"I do, and I am. My grandparents are there, and an uncle, some great-aunts, and assorted relatives. I can't talk to them as my Chinese is very limited, but my dad keeps up with them. He's worried but, so far, they're okay."

"The pictures coming out of there on the news are . . . unsettling."

"They are, but let's not talk about that. I want to celebrate you. You did a great job, and now you can relax. Plus, you just got three more clinics." His dimples deepened again as he lifted his glass in a toast and she tapped hers to his.

They laughed and talked for almost two hours. John seemed like a genuinely good guy. He'd worked his way up to be administrator of three clinics; he shared custody of his three-year-old son with his ex-wife, and he liked dogs. Ashley could definitely see getting to know him better. He asked a lot of questions about her, too, and really seemed to listen. She was impressed that his eyes didn't stray to the games on the TVs. In her experience, most guys would have been drawn to them. Mark definitely would have.

At 10:00 p.m. he grabbed her hand and gave it a small squeeze. "Ashley, I'm really enjoying you, but I need to put the final touches on my presentation for tomorrow. Would it be okay if I call you?"

"I'd like that very much. Let me see your phone."

He swiped his phone to unlock it and handed it to her, watching as she added her number. Taking her hand, he stood. In her heels, they were the same height, so she was staring right into his brown eyes when he leaned in and kissed her cheek.

"You'll be hearing from me . . . soon." He turned and walked away, then turned back and waved his phone at her. It was the second time he'd done that, and it made her feel like a schoolgirl.

She touched her cheek where his lips had been, and her phone buzzed. Looking down she saw he'd texted her already, just a heart emoji. *Perfect.*

She was slightly disappointed he hadn't invited her up to his room, but wouldn't that be premature? She just got rid of one man she'd jumped into bed with too soon. Nope, it was better to start slow and actually get to know someone first. Yes, that was her new motto. No more bad surprises for her. She would take this slow.

CHAPTER SEVEN

Maya

February 20, 2020

I'm scared to death. There's this new virus, the coronavirus, that is getting really bad in Italy. Mom is still there helping Nonna. Dad and I are glued to the news. Nonna has had both of her hip replacements and is doing well. Dad wants Mom on the first plane home, but she already has a ticket for next week. She doesn't want to pay the stiff penalty to change it. She says it's not the money, it's the principle.

This virus is scary, but no one here is worried about it. It started in China. The president said not to worry—it's a foreign virus, a 'China virus'." I think it started with bats or something, and now it's in Italy. This morning we called Mom; Dad and I sat next to each other on the living room couch sharing the phone. It's nighttime in Italy.

"How are you, Mamma?" I use the Italian word for Mom when I'm feeling little.

"Oh Bimba," she says, calling me 'baby girl'. "I'm fine. Don't worry about me. Nonna and Nonno have a little cold. Your aunt and uncle and both cousins are just fine. Are you studying?"

"Yes," I assure her.

"Good. Now let me talk to your father."

"Okay, I love you."

"Love you more, Bimba."

Dad begs her to come home *now*. I've never heard him beg. They don't usually fight, not like Mom and I do. He just lets her have her way. Not today—today he got angry, pacing around the living room as they talked, but she is standing firm. He shoves the phone back to me and stomps off.

I feel nervous as I lift the phone to my ear. "So, you won't come home early?" My voice trembles.

But Mom is as stubborn as ever. "Why should I spend hundreds of dollars to change my ticket when I'll be home next week? I'm a doctor. I'll be fine."

She's a doctor. She'd know if she needed to come home.

"Okay. I love you, Mamma."

"I love you too, Bimba. Study hard and take care of your father. I'll be home soon. *Ciao.*"

What if she gets the virus? What if she dies and the last time we talked I slammed the door on her? She said she loved me too and would see me soon. Before she hung up, she coughed, and now I can't sleep. The virus starts with a cough.

My mind runs around in circles. Yes, I fight with my mom, but it's like she is the sun, and Dad and I circle around her like planets. She is the heart, the force that holds us together. I've never, never in my whole life, thought about what life would be like without her. My body is shaking, tired—worn out from worry. "God, please bring her home. Bring her home. I promise I'll do anything, just bring her home."

CHAPTER EIGHT

La Rue

March 2020

LaRue was glued to the television. The political turmoil was bad enough, but now there was this virus. The president has finally declared a Public Health Emergency, which he should have done weeks ago, in her opinion. Travel restrictions are in place, and more people in China have died due to covid than when the SARS epidemic happened.

What would Walter think of all this craziness? Secretly, she was glad he was gone these ten years. He would hate this. Gone so long and, still, the thought of him brought tears to her eyes. Oh, how she missed him, especially when the world was getting scary like this. He'd been a comforting presence, sturdy, steady, and logical, that was Walter.

She took a deep breath, wiped her eyes, and turned off the tube. She had to buck up. She lowered her legs from the comfy Lazy Boy chair, careful not to disturb her cat. The world was having a crisis and she needed to look on the bright side, as was her custom. Walter was gone, but she had enjoyed his company for 45 years. She wasn't worried about herself. No, at 75, she'd had a great life, had a cozy little home, and a grumpy cat she loved despite his attitude. If she died, she'd be in a better place, she knew that. Although the idea of drowning as her lungs filled with fluid was not appealing, that's how they'd described it on television. She wouldn't think of that. So what if they had to "shelter in place." She'd been doing that, in effect, for years.

Nope, she wasn't worried about herself. She peeked out of the window next to her chair at the house across the street. She was concerned about her neighbors, dear Jonathan and his sweet daughter Maya. "You should see her, Walter. That girl has sprouted up in the last year like a beanstalk, and her skin cleared up. She's almost 17, and turning into a beauty, like her mama. And she's scared to death. It's a shame."

Maya's mother was stuck in Italy with her parents, and they were all sick. On top of that, the flights had all been canceled and she couldn't get home. LaRue knew they were thinking the worst, and yet, either Jonathan or Maya came over to check on her every day. *Every day!* She adored them. They were like family to her, and they were hurting. That's what kept her up at night. There was nothing she could do to ease their pain; it was unimaginable. Sophia is beautiful, fiery, and passionate. She loves her family and worries constantly about Maya. Now, what will happen?

"And what about that little gal next door, the one with the dogs? What was her name? Amber? No, Ashley. She was what . . . maybe 30? Whatever happened to that guy she lived with? Good riddance, I say, Walter. You wouldn't have liked him. He was the kind of guy who would smile to your face one minute, then run into your garbage can and drive off the next." One night she heard a huge racket. She got out of bed and looked out the window. He was out there throwing things around and cussing. Maybe Ashley finally tossed him out. Good riddance to bad rubbish.

Ashley was attractive too, in a girl-next-door kind of way, with her hair pulled back in a ponytail, and sweatpants. She was thoughtful enough to wave whenever she took the dogs out for a run. That was the only time her car left the driveway these days. She must be working from home. "Wait," she said out loud. "Isn't she a nurse? Oh dear, I wonder how she's doing during this crazy time. Doctors and nurses are getting the worst of this virus. Hospitals are filling up and respirators are in tight demand."

And how about others around the world, especially those Syrian refugees all smashed together in tent camps, and half of them children? What if the virus gets into that refugee camp; or a prison; or those poor children at the border? "And the church is closed, Walter! The service is on Zoom. Who is feeding the homeless now? Or are they going without?"

She'd done it again. It was hard to keep her mind from going down the rabbit hole of bad thoughts, and that ridiculous president of ours was making everything worse. She was happy Walter didn't live long enough to see this. It would have killed him. *He's probably been flipping like a pancake in the grave since the last election.* She smiled to herself. Well, if you couldn't laugh about it, you'd cry.

She wasn't young anymore, and some of the time her arthritis kept her home. Except for church and lunch afterward with her friends, or an occasional trip to the store or the hairdresser, her life under quarantine hadn't changed that much. She would miss her friends, they had to move their "girl's night" to Zoom after Jackie figured out how to work it, and they didn't meet to make sandwiches for the homeless anymore. And she missed going to church.

When the "culture wars" started pitting people against people, she became a Methodist. "Us-vs.-Them Christianity" was not for her. Walter would have approved of her move, three years ago, away from the evangelicals. Anyway, their worship was getting too loud for her. The fog machine had been the last straw. What was this; a rock concert or a worship service?

"Anyway, Walter, Methodists are quieter." Even though she didn't understand all the rituals, she rather liked their liturgy and the prayers. She missed her friends, though. Betty had COPD, and Jackie, although the healthiest of the three of them, had asthma, so they both had to be very careful. She should call them today. What if they got the virus? "Oops, it happened again, down the rabbit hole I go. There's only one thing for it."

She pushed herself out of her chair, knocking Hershey to the floor and receiving a dirty look from him. She limped down the hall into the little room she thought of as the prayer room. She found the lighter, lit a candle, picked up her notebook, and sat in her recliner. It was here that she could do some good. At least she hoped so. And, if nothing else, it helped her feel better. She pulled her reading glasses off the top of her head onto her nose, opened her notebook, and began to write out her prayers.

CHAPTER NINE

Ashley

March 2020

Ashley was depressed, no doubt about it. Being stuck inside because of this virus was already getting to her. Time to walk the dogs. She pulled on her fleece jacket and laced up her hiking boots. Of course, it would snow in March. It was Reno. They'd had the mildest winter, then, suddenly, just when the Shelter in Place—order came, the snow had fallen. Today looked overcast, but dry and cold. Pepper and Westly danced around her as she tied her bootlaces. They knew what boots meant; they were going for a hike. It hadn't even been a week since they'd been told to stay home, and she already felt like a caged animal. At least she was allowed to go out with the dogs. What would she do without the dogs?

A large part of her sadness came from John. Their relationship had started like water gushing through a funnel. They had long phone conversations several nights in a row. Talking and flirting with him made her feel young and free. He'd signed up his clinics with her company and they'd set up her first training for February. She couldn't wait to see him in person again.

Then the virus hit Washington State. It swept through entire retirement homes like a tempest not that far from John. Their conversations shrunk to short Marco Polo videos that came every few days.

"Ash, did you hear? A nursing facility in Kirkland, which is only four hours from us, is full of covid. Twenty-seven of the residents and something like 25 of the staff have symptoms." He sounded disconsolate.

"Ash, I'm going to need to homeschool Ky. I'm terrified. How am I supposed to do that and run the clinics? Kate and I will have to split it, and we're not the best at working things out together."

And "Ash, I've had to cancel all elective procedures. Our clinics are full of covid patients. We're not built for this."

She could tell he was a mess. His usually perfect hair was mussed and dark circles showed under his eyes. He looked like he hadn't slept in a week. There was nothing she could do to help him.

Then the communication shrank to a

trickle, with an occasional text.

"Ash, I may have to close the clinics. Elective procedures are our bread and butter. How can we stay open?"

And then this. "Ash, my dad can't get ahold of our relatives in China."

The next text delivered the final blow. "Ash, I really like you, but right now I need to focus on my family and this virus. I just can't think of anything else. I'm sorry. Maybe in the future. I hope so." She had not heard from him again.

Mark was gone. The last she heard, he'd moved on to some other unsuspecting woman. She thought about sending her an anonymous cautionary message but decided against it. Now her short-lived relationship with John was over. Dang, life sucks!

Pepper's whining brought her back to the present. She locked the front door and headed out to her bright red Honda Element, the dogs leaping and dancing all the way. She held open the back hatch, the dogs jumped in, and she shivered. Maybe she should have brought her thicker gloves. The sky above her was gray, but no snow yet. The outside thermometer read 27°, but she'd gotten used to that. Coming from the Bay Area, Reno's seasons had been a bit of a shock.

Glancing up, she saw old Mrs. Zollinger in the window waving. She waved back and climbed into the car. Poor lady, all alone. She didn't even have dogs to keep her company, just an ancient cat.

It was a short drive to the entrance of Evan's Canyon, where the dogs could run off-leash. She loved the beauty and desolation of the high desert, so different from San Francisco, but working from home was no fun. She missed the travel to all the western states in her region, and her colleagues, though they often drove her crazy.

Ashley pulled into the parking area of her favorite hiking spot. The trail was muddy. *Ugh,* she hated hiking in the mud. It was good she'd opted for boots; there would be no running today. Slogging was more like it.

Tugging her headwrap to cover her ears, she opened the back hatch. The dogs took off in a flash, sniffing and exploring, pooping almost immediately. She used her biodegradable doggy bags to pick up the poop and tied them closed, then tossed them in the conveniently placed trash receptacle. Her body warmed after about a mile on the path that snaked through the sagebrush. She was glad she'd opted for her lighter gloves after all.

A couple was hiking toward her. Thankfully, their dogs were off-leash, so she didn't have to tie up her own. She never understood people who leashed their dogs out here. Dogs on leashes are territorial. They're much nicer when they can greet each other the way dogs like to do. She moved to one side to let the couple pass. They stopped a few yards away to chat. People were supposed to stay six feet apart and wear masks, but outside, it didn't seem logical. She did have one in her pocket, and these folks wore theirs dropped down around their necks. She felt her body relax. It would be nice to talk to someone.

The couple was older, maybe in their 50s. Their two hound dogs chased around with Pepper and Westly. She was glad to see her dogs get some running in. They got bored in her small condo.

The woman laughed as the hounds started to bay. "They needed this."

"Mine too," agreed Ashley. "How old are yours?"

"They're sisters, about four years old," said the fellow. "What kind of dogs are yours?"

"Well, I got them both at the Humane Society, so I'm not positive. Pepper, the black one, was listed as a lab and border collie mix, a 'Borador' they said."

"Both active breeds," said the man.

"Yep, and he's only three, so he has a lot of energy. Westly is about five, but I don't know what breed he is."

The man studied Westly. "I think there might be some Weimaraner in there."

"Others have said that, maybe mixed with beagle. I don't know. He's got the mischievousness of a beagle, that's for sure." She laughed.

"Well," said the lady, "nice chatting with you. Stay safe."

"You too." Ashley felt slightly disappointed the conversation ended so soon. She definitely needed human contact. Maybe Mrs. Zollinger next door... *I bet she's lonely, and she can't have been exposed to the virus because she never goes anywhere.* She turned to continue her hike. Not for the first time, she missed Mark. No, that wasn't right, she did not miss Mark, he was a jerk, and she stayed with him too long as it was, but she missed the *idea* of Mark. The comfort of having someone to come home to and discuss your day, especially now. But the thought of being quarantined with Mark made her shiver. She walked faster. John—she missed John, although it was really just the idea of John that she missed too. All the hopes and dreams she'd let herself have.

She snapped back to the present as Pepper barked and ran on up the trail. As she rounded the bend, someone was coming her way. Her dogs ran off to say hello. The closer she got, she could see it was a guy, and it looked like he had only one dog, some kind of husky . . . thankfully, not leashed.

Again, she stopped to chat. "Great day for a hike," he said. He was tall, athletic, and handsome.

"Agreed," she said, gesturing to the dogs. "We needed to get out."

"Us too. Couldn't take it much longer, I'm not used to being inside. Good thing it's only for a month. How are you holding up?"

She liked the way people looked out for each other during this crisis, even if it was from a "safe distance." It was the goodness of people that she saw more often than not, except for the damn toilet paper hoarders. "I'm okay. Working from home. How about you?"

"Me too. I did IT at the Atlantis, but I'm at home now. They closed the casino, but thankfully I still have a job. I just work and sit at home unless I'm out here. It's maddening. What do you do?"

"I'm a nurse." He flinched, so she rushed on. "Don't worry, I'm not in patient care. I train nurses and docs in preventive health care . . . well, I did. Things are pretty slow on that end right now. Everyone's resources have gone to covid." Would he think less of her for not rushing to the hospital to help? She struggled with this daily.

He laughed. "I imagine. I'm Parker, by the way. I'd shake your hand, but . . . you know." When he grinned, she saw he had a cleft in his chin, and for some reason, it made her blush.

"Ashley." Although desperate to keep him talking, she was suddenly at a loss for words.

He watched the dogs chasing in and out of the sagebrush. "They seem happy. Jasmine loves to play-chase."

"Your dog's name is *Jasmine?*" That almost made her giggle, but she stifled it. People could be very sensitive about their dogs, but she'd never heard of a dog named after a Disney Princess. Especially a guy's dog.

He grinned at her. *"Princess* Jasmine, to be exact. My niece called her that, and it just stuck."

A warm flush crept up Ashley's chest at that. He liked his niece enough to let her name his dog Jasmine. Such a sweet thing to do.

He stood with his arms crossed, seeming content to watch the dogs play.

Maybe he was lonely too. She wondered if he wore a ring under his gloves. She strategically slipped her gloves off and brushed back a loose strand of hair so he could see she didn't.

"Well, Ashley, it's been nice meeting you." He grinned and said in a lounge-lizard way, "So, do you come here often?"

She laughed at the obvious pick-up line. "I do. Mostly about this time of the morning."

"Well, hopefully, I'll see you tomorrow."

She turned to continue her hike, grinning from ear to ear.

Chapter Ten

Maya

March 15th, 2020

They're gone. All of them.

Dad and I were just waking up when Mom's brother Sergio called. Dad set his coffee down on the kitchen island and put the phone on speaker.

Mostly, my uncle just sobbed. "*Morto, tutti e tre*—dead, all three," he kept saying. "Nothing we could do..." Dad clicked the phone off speaker and walked away. I stood there in my robe like a lost lamb in a forest full of wolves. I knew something terrible had happened, but I didn't know what. Did Nonna or Nonno die? When Dad came back into the kitchen he told me that all three had died—Mom, and both of her parents. I didn't believe him. Not for a long time. It couldn't be true.

I remember it like a montage from a movie. Dad holding me, me shaking and sinking to the floor, me wailing, "No, no, no." His tears falling on my hair. It was like the world had just stopped spinning. We were holding onto each other so we didn't fall off.

"Everyone will lose someone during the pandemic." That's what the news anchor said.

I feel like I've lost the most. Practically my whole family. As I mentioned, my grandparents, Nonna and Nonno, live in Italy, and my mom was there helping my grandma, who was having both hips replaced. They are all gone now, and we can't even fly there to bury them or go to their funeral. Italy is on the covid-banned list. The worst part is we didn't get to say goodbye, just a phone call with my mom, who was coughing a lot. Dad is distraught; so am I.

I guess that's why Dad has been so strict about not letting me leave the house now that the virus has hit the US. He kept me home from school the Friday before the schools even closed. I'm all he has left now, except his brother's family. His parents, my other grandparents, live in New York, so we hardly ever get to see them.

I'm sitting on my bed in my room, in the dark, where I've been all week. Everyone has to stay in their house. The governor had a press conference and told all non-essential workers to stay home. Now they're saying this could go on for months. We're all trying to "flatten the curve" so we don't become like Italy. By that they mean, if everyone gets sick at once, the hospitals won't have enough ventilators, so people will die in the hallways, and the doctors will have to decide who to save. The news videos of hospital hallways lined with patients are terrifying.

That thought makes me sick to my stomach. Mom was a doctor. What if she had to decide which kid to save and which to let die? How do you even make that decision?

I picture my mom standing in her white coat in a hospital hallway staring at two gurneys. On one is a child, on another is an 80-year-old, but there is only one ventilator. Is a child's life more important than an older person's? Do they choose the healthier person or the famous one? The rich one over the poor one? These are crazy-making questions.

So, if we all stay home, fewer people will get sick at once, and maybe more folks can live. I'm glad Mom and my grands died at their home; not in some hospital hallway. At least there's that.

Wow, I'm rambling. My brain is bouncing around like a pinball. I can't keep one thought for very long. Theoretically, it's spring break at school anyway, so I don't have to do homework. Even that thought hurts. If Mom were here, she'd make me do some anyway. My history teacher asked us to write a journal. He said we should be keeping track of what happens during the pandemic, so I decided to be better about keeping this journal. It gives me something to do. I went back and read what I wrote before. It seems like a lifetime ago. I wrote that the fight on my first day of school was the worst thing that ever happened to me. What a joke. This is way worse. Now I feel sick most of the time. I can't sleep. I know Dad's not sleeping either; he has black smudges under his eyes. It's hard to eat. At dinner, we both push food around on our plates.

The last time I spoke to Mom in person, I slammed the door. I *slammed* the door!

I can't even go over to see LaRue. I call her a lot though. She just listens when I cry.

CHAPTER ELEVEN

Maya

March 26th, 2020

My covid-19 Virus Journal

I'm sitting on my bed in my room writing this on my silver Dell computer. I don't really leave my bed these days.

My name is Maya Hunter, and I'm a 16-year-old senior in high school. I know that's weird; I'll explain it later. My room is cozy with lots of browns, greens, and reds. Mom decorated it for me. It's very Italian—lush in fabrics and colors. It's cold out today. Spring in Reno is very unpredictable. I'm snuggled under my soft plush comforter. We live in a big old Victorian house which now feels empty.

All that work Mom did, all that school, and moving, and . . . for what? She's gone now. She was a great doctor. It breaks my heart in so many ways. I miss her and can't even do anything about it. I even miss fighting with her.

Anyway, I didn't mind moving from Pennsylvania because, well, I just never really fit in there. And it was cold too. And I'm crazy about my Aunt Nancy and Uncle Todd who have my only three cousins in America. They are younger than me; I love them. Penelope and Violet are eleven and eight. Everett is five, and so stinkin' cute!

Frankly, I was ready for a fresh start my senior year in Reno and, after the fight and all, things were looking up for a good senior year, which, you may have surmised, is wrecked again. No senior cut day, no football games, no prom, no graduation—probably. That's a lot to let go of. I may as well just call 2020 a lost year and skip off to college. I had big hopes for this year too, as I mentioned earlier–getting a boyfriend and all, which seemed possible with Sam. Now, with SIP, I can't even leave the house to see him.

So, anyway, we moved here, and we found the coolest house. It's huge and old, like really old—120 years old. But it's been all remodeled with refinished wood floors and cream-colored walls. I love thinking about all the people who lived here before us and what their lives were like. Now I wonder if we will even be able to keep this house. Seems like everything is up in the air now. . *Sigh*. I feel like I sigh a lot now.

Mom was, as I have mentioned, beautiful. She is, was, 100 percent Italian and had black hair and eyes, and a fiery personality. Dad says I'm a lot like her, though I don't see it. She liked Reno, too, because Italian ranchers had settled the part of the city we live in, and a lot of the old families here have Italian names. Mom was – *intense*. There is no other way to describe her. And there was no way she was going to stay home when her parents asked her to come help them. When Mom made up her mind about something, she was as unmovable as a boulder. She planned to talk them into moving in with us, which is why we bought this big house. It would have been so fun to have Nonno and Nonna here. Nonno had a great laugh, and Nonna was the best cook—her homemade raviolis were my favorite. I just can't believe they are gone.

My relationship with Mom was – *complicated.* I feel like I'm repeating myself. She always pushed me hard. I started Kindergarten at four and I actually skipped sixth grade because she didn't want me to be bored, but she made me work hard for that. And that's why I'm the only 16-year-old senior I know of. I'll be seventeen in June, though. I was shy and didn't want to skip a grade, but I guess getting to college early will be good.

So, Mom went to Italy. We knew about the virus in China, but it was still new, so we didn't know much about it. And it was all the way over in China! She was supposed to stay for a month or so, until Nonna healed, and then bring Nonna and Nonno back with her. But, in that short time, Italy got smacked hard with the Coronavirus. The Italian government didn't move fast enough, and covid-19 spread like lightning. That really pisses me off.

One time I asked Dad why the Italians took so long to respond to the pandemic. It was one night after dinner, when sometimes I can get him to talk.

"That's the way Italians are," he said. "They are very slow to react, and very present-oriented." He got a far-away look in his eye, like he was thinking of Mamma. "When I went to Italy to meet your mom's family, I noticed how the people lived in the moment. They weren't really thinking about the future, just enjoying the food, the wine, the conversation. It was beautiful."

Dad drifts off like he's lost in thought, and I picture Mom and Nonna and Nonno eating and drinking and not paying attention to what is happening around them. And suddenly everyone is dying.

Dad is the strong silent type. He's half-Italian, but more the New York version. I think his other half is English or something. He fought hard to get Mom to come home. It was the first time I ever heard him get angry with her. He's still mad. He kind of moves through the house like an angry ghost. I mostly stay out of his way. But if she had come home, would she have spread the virus to the people on the plane and even brought it home to us?

That's all I can write today. I need sleep.

Well, the governor dropped the hammer this week. He actually yelled at people who weren't taking the Close-your-non-essential-business thing seriously. He may start fining people who refuse to shut their businesses down. Our governor is a middle-aged white guy with gray hair. I feel really bad for him and all the governors. Every decision they make seems to make people mad. Dad and I sat together in the living room last night, watching him on the news when the governor yelled, "You don't understand. People will DIE!" Dad and I just looked at each other. You don't have to tell *us*.

"I'm glad he's taking it seriously," said Dad. Dad's a Republican, but he's confused about people's response to this virus.

Me too.

The news from Italy keeps getting worse. Higher death-counts every day.

I can't stop thinking about all the people who are losing their jobs. In Nevada, they closed all the casinos, which put over 200,000 people out of work. The government is promising monetary relief, but I just don't see how all those people will survive. If Dad has to stop work, how long can we make it? We're not a two-income family anymore.

My mind circles around these negative thoughts like water down a drain, so I've decided to try to think about at least one good thing a day. So, here is my one happy thing for today: Sam and I are sending snaps back and forth on Snapchat when I get this question: "Can I get your number so we can text?"

My stomach filled with butterflies when I read that. So now we're texting as well as snapping. It makes the day go faster to share it with somebody. I text with Shannon too, and sometimes we play games online, but she seems to be losing interest. It's like everybody is pulling into their own cocoon or something.

Dad is still working. Being a construction worker, I guess it's okay because he's outside all day. They say it's safer outside.

Dad says, "The governor won't stop construction because in Las Vegas they are building a stadium for the Oakland Raiders."

He means the Las Vegas Raiders. Whatever. Still, it makes me worry. If I lost him, I'd be alone. What would happen to me? Especially now that the travel bans are on. His folks live in New York, which is not a great place to be right now. It's getting hit big time with the covid virus. If they die, and Dad dies...This is scary, like one of those dystopian novels, only this is extremely real. I guess I could live with my aunt and uncle. There goes my swirling-poop-brain again.

I do better if I don't look at the news. Most of the time I read, watch reruns on TV, or play on my phone. There's this crazy TV show about a guy who has a zoo full of tigers. It's like watching a train wreck. Dad and I are binge-watching it at night. At least it gives us something to talk about besides the virus. We sit on the couch, eat popcorn, and laugh. Sometimes I feel guilty about laughing when my mom just died. But it feels good too. It's the strangest show, but everyone is watching. School was supposed to start next week. Then they said we get another week of Spring Break. Then they started talking about maybe having school online. California shut all their schools for the rest of the year. I'm going to die a virgin; I just know it.

CHAPTER TWELVE

LaRue

March 2020

Finally, here was something she could do to help, besides pray and listen to dear Maya cry on the phone. She shook her head just thinking about the girl and her father. The worst had happened and her heart could barely hold more pain. Others at church were sick too. It was an older congregation and she couldn't help but worry.

One of the women from her book club emailed a simple pattern to make masks, since we all needed to wear them now. There was a huge shortage of masks since they all came from China, which is now locked down with covid, and people were hoarding them. "These wouldn't help the doctors," she informed Walter. "They need a special kind of mask, but they might help the patients who need to wear masks, so they don't cough or sneeze on other people."

LaRue got to work at once. As a quilter, she had stacks of material and lots of time to sew them, as much as her arthritis would allow. On the first day she made ten, the second day, sixteen. They were easy to make once she got the hang of it and because she liked to make cheerful quilts, all of her quilting fabrics were bright and colorful. But how would she get them down to the hospital?

The answer came right then as Ashley's car pulled into the driveway next door. LaRue went to the window and opened it. Today was much warmer than it had been for a while, in the 50°s, she guessed. She'd normally be in the yard getting the flower beds ready, but the masks seemed more important.

"Ashley!" She waved frantically.

Ashley stopped. The dogs jumped out of the car and followed her into LaRue's front yard. "You okay, Mrs. Zollinger?"

"I'm fine, dear, but I need a favor."

Those dogs of hers were sniffing around the yard. She hoped they wouldn't make a mess on her lawn.

As if she could read LaRue's mind, Ashley said, "How about I put the dogs in and come over?"

"That would be lovely, dear." She enjoyed being old enough to call everyone *dear* and get away with it. That way, if she forgot their names it didn't matter.

She watched the pretty girl disappear into her house. LaRue dashed around the house picking up, folding her throw blanket and laying it over the back of the couch, plumping pillows, and giving the coffee table a quick dusting with a tissue. Ashley wasn't a girl, actually; she was a grown woman. But everyone looked like a girl to LaRue. First, it was the doctors who looked like children, then the pilots, and now it was *everyone*. Ashley was a nurse. Maybe she shouldn't be talking to her; nurses are exposed to covid every day. She didn't really know her. They'd only had a few short conversations, and LaRue didn't want to risk being exposed.

Ashley came back out of her house quickly and over to LaRue's, her brown ponytail tossing as she walked.

LaRue opened the door before she could knock and noticed that Ashley had stepped back several feet from the door. Probably keeping the 6'-Rule, which was smart. Silly of her to think the girl would want to come in.

"How are you feeling, Mrs. Zollinger?"

"Oh, I'm fit as a fiddle, dear. Thanks for coming over. It's just that I'm making masks for the hospital and I was wondering if, one time when you're at work, if you'd drop them off for me?"

"Oh, I don't work in a hospital, thank goodness. I work from home."

LaRue took a deep breath, relieved. The hospitals were a mess just now. *But how the dickens can a nurse work from home? Wouldn't she need to be where the patients are?*

"But that's really nice of you to make the masks. I'd be glad to drop them off." Ashley gave LaRue the biggest smile.

To LaRue, that smile felt like liquid sunshine. Ashley had a lovely smile. Like that actress, Julia Roberts', it took up most of her face.

"That's great, just let me get them, dear." LaRue left the door open when she went to get the paper sack she'd put masks in. She handed it out to Ashley, who seemed to hesitate.

"Dear, I haven't been out of the house in weeks; I promise you I'm well."

"Of course." Ashley stepped up and took the bag, looking inside. "Those are great. So fun and colorful."

"Well, I'm a quilter."

"They're great," she repeated, then, as if she remembered something, "Mrs. Zollinger, do you need me to get you groceries or anything?"

"Oh, that is so thoughtful, dear, but Jonathan brings me what I need. But, if you could come back in a couple of days, I'll have more masks, I'm sure."

"Jonathan? Is that your...son?"

LaRue shook her head, blinking back tears as her throat started to swell. She cleared it, "No dear, we didn't have any children. Jonathan..." she pointed at the house across the street, "... lives over there with his daughter. Sweet man." She couldn't talk about them right now. She knew she'd burst into tears.

"Oh, right. Well, I'd be glad to take the masks. It makes me feel like I can do something useful. I feel so . . . helpless, ya know?"

"I know exactly what you mean. Now you take care, and stay well, okay?"

"You bet. And I'll come back in a couple of days for some more masks."

"Thank you, dear, and please call me LaRue."

The girl looked down like she was trying to decide if she could do that. "Okay, LaRue, thank you."

LaRue shut the door and smiled. She was doing something to help, besides praying, of course, and she felt a bit more spring in her step. She'd better call "the girls" and check in on them too. This was not the time to wallow; this was the time for action.

CHAPTER THIRTEEN

Ashley

March 2020

Taking the dogs on a walk had become the best part of Ashley's day. Parker conveniently met her at the parking area, and they headed out together, six feet apart, of course, but because they were outside they didn't wear masks. Today he was waiting for her. It sent a thrill through her. He'd been good about keeping his distance, walking ahead on the single track, but today he started asking questions, and she knew what he was trying to discern.

"So, how long have you been staying home?" he asked, sounding casual.

"Been a couple weeks now. You?"

"Same." He kept a good pace. The mud had started to dry out, and soon she'd be able to run again, but she was worried about that.

"Hey," she took a breath for courage. "Uh, I'm usually running up here when it's not muddy. You wouldn't be a runner, would you?"

He laughed. "I can run."

She thought he sounded happy that she'd asked.

He continued his interrogation. "So, you feel well, no sore throat or cough, no fever." He was getting right to it now, no more beating around the bush.

"Healthy," she said. "You?"

"Same." As the single trail widened to a double track, he dropped back next to her for the first time. "So, you think we can risk being closer than six feet?"

She grinned. "I thought you'd never ask." They both laughed. This was dating in the time of covid-19. All the rules had changed.

"Good," he said, sounding relieved. "Um ... could I get your email so I can invite you to a virtual happy hour tonight?"

Chills ran up her spine. He was interested in her. This was the best thing that had happened to her since being sent home to work. "Sure," she said. "I can text it to you." She smiled to herself, thinking that was a sly way to get his number. She had a lot of questions she'd love to ask him over a glass of wine.

"Great," he said. "Several of my friends started doing this online last week, so I thought I'd invite you to join us."

A lump formed in her throat. Still she tried not to let the disappointment show on her face. "Great," she said. *Am I just "one of the gang" then? Or worse, someone he feels sorry for? Maybe he has a girlfriend and I will meet her tonight on the computer.* Dark thoughts assailed her as they transitioned back to a single track, and she was lost in them all the way back to the car.

At the parking lot, she handed him her phone and he typed in his number. He smiled his strong-chin smile and waved as he loaded Jasmine into his pickup and drove toward the exit, then slowed, leaning out the window with a See-you-tonight goodbye.

She was overthinking this. He was gorgeous, kind, and fun. But what did she really know about him?

He could be married, for all she knew. She'd still never seen his hands without gloves. When they talked at all, it was mostly about the virus or the dogs. Mark had been charming at first too, she reminded herself.

At home, she herded the dogs into the house and then went to check on Mrs. Zollinger. *I mean, LaRue.* She'd been raised by Midwesterners who had trained her to greet her elders respectfully, which meant using Mr., Miss, or Mrs. It had been a hard habit to break when her family moved to San Francisco, but the west was a much more casual culture; no one did that here.

She hadn't stopped by in a few days. LaRue was sewing masks as fast as she could, and the lady at the drop-off checkpoint seemed delighted to get them. It made Ashley feel slightly less guilty about not volunteering to work in the hospital.

The door opened before she got to the stoop. LaRue smiled at her with her sparkling blue eyes. "I'm glad you came by, dear. I have a big bag for you today. And Jonathan brought me some avocados, but I can't eat that many so I thought I'd share with you."

LaRue handed out two bags—one full of masks and one of avocados. "Thank you." Ashley took the masks but hesitated about the other bag.

"Oh, don't worry dear, they are healthy. I wish I could say the same for his wife and her parents, though."

"Oh no, what happened?"

"His wife was a doctor, you know, and she went to Italy to take care of her folks, and all three died of the virus."

"That's terrible." Ashley's stomach tightened at the news. It put her troubles in perspective.

"And that little girl of his—she's only sixteen—she's a wreck. He is too, but they hide it well. They come over every day to check on me."

"That is just the saddest thing." Ashley felt she should go, but it was hard to leave after hearing something so horrible about her neighbors. She'd seen them come and go, of course, but hadn't given them much thought. Should she do something . . . say something to them? She didn't know. Maybe she'd send flowers or take them her Taco Casserole.

"Well, dear, come again in a few days if you can. I'll keep going till my hands give out, or they tell me to stop, whichever comes first."

"Thank you, Mrs. . . . I mean, LaRue. And thanks for telling me about Jonathan and his daughter. What's her name?"

"It's Maya, dear. Sweet kid. Very thin now, though, and looks rather pale these days. It's the saddest thing."

"Yes," she agreed. "Well, I'd better be going. I've got a Zoom meeting for work. See you soon, and thanks for the masks and the avocados." She took the second bag and headed home. She'd deliver the masks later today. Her body ached with the loss her neighbors must feel. Then again, there was nothing she could do for them. Nothing that would bring back their wife and mother. She had never felt so helpless.

CHAPTER FOURTEEN

Maya

March 31, 2020

I sit cross-legged on the bed in my pajamas, smooth my hair, and turn on my computer. It's time for school. It's a bit of a joke, really. Some classes don't even meet, and for most, it's like a five-minute roll call and a packet of assignments to print out. I'm disappointed. I thought a teacher would actually be teaching, at least, or maybe I'd get to see some of my classmates' faces for more than roll call.

As the virtual classroom comes on the screen, I scan the faces. Everyone looks rumpled and tired and some of my classmates won't even turn on their video cameras—maybe they don't wear pajamas. Mine are just pajama bottoms and a T-shirt, so I can get away with it. Maybe they don't want us to see their hair all mussy. I don't even care anymore.

After roll call, my History teacher says, "I have an announcement. Good news: we are supposed to go back to school on May 1st."

Kids perk up then, but Anil Sandhu raises his virtual hand and Mr. Harrison calls on him.

"My dad says, don't count on getting back to school anytime soon."

Well, that brings down the mood. We all groan, and Anil shrugs as if to say, "Hey, I'm only the messenger." Anil's dad is on the school board, but I'm holding onto hope that we can go back. There's little enough of that around our house. Dad is now worried about his folks, 'cause they live in New York and it's a disaster there too. On TV they show mobile morgues, and coffins being put into giant mass graves. Dad usually changes the channel. But we know about it 'cause we talk to Grandpa and Grandma a lot. They are staying inside. My uncle says he and his family might head to New York just to be sure.

Anyway, the best part of school being online is that the fight I had the first week is the last thing on anyone's mind now. We'll all just be so glad when we get to see each other again. They're not even teaching us anything new, only reviewing what we already know. I guess, as a senior, it's not too bad. College admissions look at the tests we took last year. I'll be going to our local college anyway. I was looking outside the state, but it would be too hard on Dad if I left town now.

Hold on, there's a woodpecker or something at my window, and it's making me crazy.

OMG. You're not going to believe this. It's not a woodpecker. It's SAM! I'm telling you this like you were here.

So, he's standing out in my yard below my window in his warm coat, and he's holding these placards and grinning. His mask is down around his neck. He holds the placards up so I can see them. The first one says, in BIG capital letters,

"IF…"

That's all it says. He throws it on the ground and turns up the next one.

"THERE IS A PROM…"

Now my heart starts thumping. OMG, is he going to invite me to the prom?

"WILL YOU GO…"

Don't leave me hanging here, Sam. He grins and finally throws that one down to the ground.

"WITH ME?" The last one says. He stands there, smiling, his eyes sparkling at me.

Now, I'm going to make *him* wait. I'm jumping up and down inside, but I leave the window to find a giant marker and some paper and scrawl my answer in huge letters. I look out the window. He shuffles his feet like he's getting anxious, and I can't stand it. I hold up my sign.

"YES!!!" (With three exclamation points).

He grins and throws down his sign and does a happy dance like he just made a touchdown, which makes me laugh so hard. I push open my window.

"Hi," I say, suddenly shy, which is silly, but we haven't talked in person in weeks.

"Hi," he says, looking like he feels the same way.

"So, this prom…" I begin, "…if it happens. Tell me more about it. I've never been to a school dance. I only know proms from movies."

"You haven't?" His mouth drops open as if he's genuinely shocked. "Why not? Guys must have been lining up to take you."

I can tell he means it, and now my throat feels tight, and I have to take some slow breaths. I've never been the girl guys fight over, that's for sure. I shrug. "We moved a lot," is my lame answer. But what he doesn't know is that I've always been the girl on the outside looking in. The girl with no real friends, that guys never notice. The quiet one.

"Maybe they were afraid of you," he says with a wicked grin. "I hear you pack a mean punch."

I want to throw something at him, but there's a window screen between us. I pick up my tape dispenser and hold it menacingly in the air.

He pretends to duck. "Whoa, calm down now. Don't make me regret the invitation."

I put the tape down, wishing I could touch him.

"I wish I could hug you," he says as if reading my mind. We stand there grinning like fools. Finally, he breaks the silence. "Anyway, the prom is...I don't know. I've never been to a school dance either."

"What?" He's only the cutest and sweetest guy I know. "How can that be?"

He smiles and I don't think the pink on his cheeks is from the cold. "I guess I never met anyone I was interested in taking."

Hot lava just got poured into my stomach, and I'm ready to rip out this screen and kiss the boy, but he looks behind him.

"Well, I've got to get back, the folks are keeping me on lockdown. I just snuck out." He bends down to collect the placards.

"No," I say, and his head jerks up. "I mean. Is it okay if I keep those?"

He grins and stands the pile up next to the house, getting as close to me as he can. "Okay, beautiful. I'll see you on the phone. Facetime later?"

"Yes."

He turns toward home, stopping every few feet to turn and wave. I watch him until he's out of sight. It was just like a scene from a rom-com. I am glowing.

Then I think, I wish Mom was here to tell about this. But would she have even let me go? For sure she'd give me a lecture about putting school before boys. I sigh, I'm not going to think about that right now. I've been asked to the prom!

CHAPTER FIFTEEN

LaRue

April 2020

LaRue had a plan for the day. She'd take a break from sewing and clean the pantry. She liked to arrange everything by date, so the things that would expire first were in front. She'd been neglecting this task, but she just couldn't face the sewing machine this morning. It was time.

She was in the pantry on a step stool, arranging her supplies. "It's my parent's fault, as you always said, Walter." She looked at the packed shelves. Her parents had lived through the Great Depression and she had inherited some of their quirkier traits. One was to always keep a year's supply of food and paper products on hand. "Like I need all this stuff," she said. "But you know, a lot of people think it's wise to have a full pantry, now that we can't go anywhere. The only thing I need is the fresh fruits and veggies Jonathan brings me, and if worst comes to worst, I can live off these cans and share them with the neighbors."

As she stepped down a sharp pain streaked up her right leg. "Ouch, dang it. I must have stepped wrong." She stood in the pantry, trying to get a sense of the extent of her injury. She hadn't stepped on anything. "Oh, the joys of aging. You can hurt yourself by doing nothing." She could put weight on it, but when she did, it hurt.

She limped into the kitchen and took out a package of frozen peas. "I'll just elevate and ice it. It's probably fine." She hobbled into the living room and pushed her cat off the chair. Looking none too happy about that, Hershey took up a seat on the couch, his tail twitching in agitation.

LaRue put her leg up on the ottoman and wrapped the towel around the peas. "That ought to do it." She clicked on the TV and found a rerun of *Mash*.

That afternoon, when she saw Jonathan's truck pull into the driveway, she made the call she'd been dreading. His feet dragged as he walked to the house. It had been like this since Sophia died. She knew he'd been working since the wee hours, and he was surely hungry and ready for a nap. But really, what choice did she have?

He answered on the second ring just as he stepped into his house. "Hello."

"Hi, hon, it's LaRue."

"Oh hi," he said, sounding as weary as he looked.

"I really hate to ask you this, but I stepped wrong off my footstool today, and even with all the icing and anti-inflammatories, it's not looking very good. Might you be able to take me down for an X-ray? It's probably nothing, but I'd like to know."

"Of course." His voice was crisp, alert now and worried. "I'll just grab a sandwich and be right over."

She could hear Maya in the background. "Dad, what's wrong? Is LaRue okay? Can I go with you?"

Oh, the sweet girl. LaRue heard Jonathan tell her, "No, it's not safe out there." LaRue knew he would not be risking his daughter. She felt bad to ask him after he'd been out all day.

She rushed to assure him. "You can just drop me off at the door, no need to expose yourself. I'll call you when I'm ready for a ride home. And I've got a sandwich already made for you."

"I'll be right there." The phone clicked off and he came back out the door, getting into his truck and pulling it in a U-turn in front of her house.

She watched out the window as he came up her walk, tapped on the door, and opened it. She was thankful they had that kind of relationship. He was rather like a son to her now and they got along great . . . as long as they didn't talk politics.

"Can I look at it?" he asked.

LaRue removed the towel and the latest bag of frozen vegetables. Jonathan knelt and gingerly examined her ankle. "Hmm, definitely swelling and turning some wild colors. We'd better get you down to the X-ray."

He helped her out of the chair and into a coat. She picked up Walter's cane and handed Jonathan a small sack that she'd put on the table by the door with his sandwiches, a bottle of water, and some cookies.

"I can't believe you made me all this food on that ankle," he said.

"Oh, it was no bother." LaRue turned to the old black cat resting on the back of the couch, scowling at her. "I'll be back, Hershey. Don't you fret now."

Jonathan laughed. She knew her cat never looked fretful, only angry, he would have given the internet-famous Grumpy Cat a run for her money. She liked it when Jonathan laughed. It was rare these days.

The ride down to the Reno Orthopedic drop-in clinic was a short one, but Jonathan managed to inhale the sandwiches and the cookies and wash it all down with water before they arrived. The man worked so hard. She inspected him and saw the dark circles under his eyes. "This is fine," she said when they pulled up to the entrance. "I'll be okay going in alone."

"Not on my watch." Jonathan pulled into a parking place.

She shook her head but knew that arguing was no use. "At least, wear this," she said, pulling a mask from her coat pocket for him and one for herself.

"Good idea." He reached out a hand. "But can we trade?"

She laughed, taking the pink polka-dot one from him and handing him the blue plaid. He helped her out of the truck, up the ramp, and pulled open the door of the clinic. She was glad to see the waiting room was mostly empty. He settled in on a couch. The tables were bare of magazines, and the seats were spaced six feet apart. Probably so no one would share germs.

A woman in a mask and scrubs rushed into the room, "I'm sorry sir but you have to wait outside."

"Oh, go on home, Jonathan," said LaRue. "I'll call you when I'm ready."

"Nope, I'll wait right out there." He gestured to the parking lot. "Text me when you're done.

She shook her head as he left. She was glad to see that everyone who worked there wore masks and gloves. Since she hadn't been out of her house in three weeks she wasn't sure who was obeying that recommendation. She fiddled with her purse, maybe she shouldn't have come. It would probably have healed on its own, and now she was exposing herself and Jonathan to hospital germs.

The X-ray didn't take long, and the doctor came in quickly to read it. He had gray hair at his temples, which allowed her to relax a bit, she had trouble trusting the competency of those young ones. "Well, my dear," he said after looking carefully at the X-ray. "You are not broken. What you have here is a sprained ankle. Have you been elevating it and icing it?'

He'd called her dear. He knew her trick. "Yes, all day."

"That's great," he assured her, speaking quickly. "You have good instincts. Now, I want you to remember RICE: Rest, Ice it for about twenty minutes each time, four to eight times a day. The C is for compression, I'm going to wrap it up tight for you, that should help. And E is elevation—try to keep it above your heart, okay? You can take Ibuprofen and alternate it with Tylenol if the pain breaks through. Do you need a script for that?"

"No, I have all that. Thank you."

The doctor wrapped her up, told her to make a follow-up appointment, and sent her on her way. Not that she wanted a broken bone, but things have been so slow lately, and this was something interesting, at least. It felt good to get out of the house and talk to someone besides her cat . . . and Walter.

Oh well, back to Hershey and the TV.

Ashley

April 2020

Ashley logged onto the link for the happy hour invite five minutes late. She did not want to be the first one there, staring awkwardly at someone she didn't know. She felt embarrassed she'd spent a good half-hour deciding what to wear, above the waist anyway. Below the waist, she was in yoga pants. She'd spent extra time on her hair and makeup too.

"Well, here goes," she said to the dogs who lay on the floor by her feet, then took a breath, exhaled, and hit the link. "Oh, no." Now was not the time for Zoom to need an update. Those can take a while. But the update started automatically, and all she could do was wait. *Why am I always so anxious? This is supposed to be fun.* "It's Mark. He ruined me," she told the dogs.

Mark always got mad when she was late. Sweat pricked under her lacy white shirt and she was glad this was not an in-person group. No one would know that she was so nervous.

Finally, the computer was done updating and she was let into the Zoom room with three others. Parker, looking handsome, as usual, smiled broadly at her. This was the first time she'd seen him without a hat of some kind. His hair looked soft, thick, and brown. "Ashley, glad you could make it." He lifted a Modelo toward her. "Ashley, this is Brandon and Cheryl."

Brandon and Cheryl sat on a couch together, his arm draped casually around her as she snuggled close to him. They wore relaxed clothing. Was she over-dressed? They lifted their glasses to her. "Hi, Ashley."

Was this everyone? If so, was it like a double date? As soon as she thought it, another face blinked on. A beautiful Latina woman with dark hair and eyes. "Hello, everyone," she said. "Oh, someone new—hello, I'm Cassandra."

Parker jumped in. "Cassandra, this is Ashley, the one I told you about."

What has he told her? Is this his girlfriend? "Hi," Ashley said, feeling a bit foolish.

"Oh, the walking partner. Nice to meet you."

The walking partner? Hmm, if Cassandra is his girlfriend, he might explain me that way. Cassandra has the most amazing eyebrows. She must know how to do them herself. Everyone else is worried about their roots and nails being a mess because the beauty shops are closed, but this woman looks model-perfect.

Bing, the computer chimed as another woman joined the group, this one was blond and a bit chunky. She said something they could not hear.

"Tess, you're muted," said Brandon. Ashley smiled. She heard that phrase a lot these days.

Again, the introductions, again, the wondering who this Tess was to Parker. Ashley hated not being there in person. You can tell a lot by being in-person and seeing how two people interact, where they sit, and by watching their body language. She was in the dark here with no physical clues.

"Okay," said Parker. "Now that we are all here, let's raise a glass to being alive and -free." He held up his beer.

Ashley raised her glass of White Zin. She chose it because if it spilled on her white lace top, it'd be easier to get the stain out. *I'm very shallow and territorial,* she thought as everyone cheered and sipped their drinks. *I have no claim on this man, and he was kind enough to invite me in. I need to think about the fact that I'm alive and healthy when so many are struggling.*

"Time for updates," said Brandon. "We'll go first." He grinned at Cheryl next to him. "You may have noticed that Cheryl is not drinking wine today...." He waited.

Is she not drinking wine? Ashley hadn't noticed. She'd held up a glass mug for the toast. Ashley just assumed she liked tea or something. *Is that weird for Cheryl? Are these folks wine snobs or something?*

"No way!" squealed Tess. "A baby?"

"Yep." Brandon grinned. Then Ashley understood.

The virtual room erupted in loud applause and salutations. Brandon and Cheryl beamed. A baby was big news, although a bit concerning during a pandemic. "Aren't you afraid?" came out of her mouth before she could stop it. The virtual room grew silent, and she wanted to kick herself. Leave it to her to blurt whatever was on her mind. Mark had always hated it when she did that.

"Beg your pardon," asked Brandon.

Was he mad, or hadn't he heard her through all the cheering? Maybe she could pretend she'd said something else.

"I was kind of wondering that, too," said Tess. "I mean, I'm thrilled for you. But isn't it a little scary to be pregnant . . . you know, *now?*" Ashley could have kissed Tess.

It was Cheryl who answered this time. "It is, actually. So, thankfully, we both get to work from home. And believe it or not, most of my doctors' visits will be over Telehealth."

"That's great," Tess and Ashley said at the same time and laughed.

Ashley's shoulders relaxed. Maybe it was the wine, but she liked Brandon, Cheryl, and Tess. Cassandra was the one she still didn't know about.

After Brandon and Cheryl were thoroughly grilled about due dates and morning sickness, Brandon steered the conversation back to the group. "Okay, update from someone else now."

Parker chimed in. "I'm still working from home. Enjoying getting to know Ashley on our walks—you want to tell everyone a little about yourself, Ash?"

Ash? Has he just nicknamed me? She wasn't sure how she felt about it. John used to call her Ash, but their relationship was mostly texting and she thought it just easier to type. Was this part of being friend-zoned, or a term of affection? "Well," she began. "I'm doing okay. Actually, I have no complaints. I'm a nurse." She looked at the group as she said this. People had different responses right now to meeting nurses. Again, guilt assailed her. It would be noble to be able to say she was fighting the good fight in the hospitals. Brandon and Cheryl looked impressed, Tess raised a glass; Cassandra, a manicured eyebrow. *What does the eyebrow mean?*

"Aren't you scared?" said Tess.

"No, I work from home as more of a consultant. I feel kind of guilty that I'm not on the front lines.

The docs and nurses are working so hard. But I'm extremely grateful too. I feel like every week is completely different. We get different information and…"

Tess interrupted. "I feel that way too. Like each week is a completely different experience." Others nodded.

Ashley continued. "I don't know, most times I feel good, but I have these neighbors across the street, a guy and his teenage daughter. His wife and his in-laws in Italy all died of covid. When I found out it put me in a spiral." Was she oversharing? She didn't know these folks, but it felt good to be able to talk to someone.

"Wow," said Cheryl.

"Yikes, that's intense," added Cassandra.

Parker, who had heard this before, just nodded.

"And…" she continued, "…my older neighbor hurt her ankle, and she lives alone, and I just worry about her. So, I guess what I'm trying to say is I'm doing great, but the state of the world and the pain of my neighbors is making me really sad."

Parker had the sweetest lift to his eyebrows like he wanted to comfort her. At least that's what she thought was happening. Online it was sometimes hard to tell where people were looking.

"I agree," said Tess. "I can't even watch the news. First, China, then Italy, Korea, Washington, and now New York. It's depressing. It makes me appreciate my little apartment, you know."

The evening went on with more updates and stories, and she even had another glass of wine, which may have been a mistake. After they all said goodbye, her phone beeped, and it was Parker asking for a FaceTime visit. She happily picked up.

"Hey," he said grinning. "I'm glad you got to meet my friends."

"They're very nice," she said. "I hope I wasn't too 'Debbie Downer' tonight."

"No," he said quickly. "I liked the things you shared. It took the conversation to deeper levels than normal. Since we've known each other a long time it's easy to stay shallow."

She sighed happily. "Cassandra's job sounds interesting." She couldn't help it. She had to fish for information.

"Marketing?" he shrugged as if 'interesting' wasn't the right word. "I guess."

The wine was making her bold. "So, how do you know her, and Tess, and Brandon and Cheryl, for that matter."

He grinned. "Brandon and I go way back. To high school, actually. He's my best friend. The other two I met through Cheryl. She worked with them, waitressing when they were all in college."

"Are you...have you...dated either of them?" She held her breath. It was better to know sooner than later.

He laughed again. "Well, not for lack of Cheryl's trying to fix me up." He shrugged. "Just not interested, I guess."

Giddiness ran up her spine.

It was his turn to fidget. "So, how about you? Dating anyone?"

She shrugged, without John, her almost-boyfriend in Washington, there was no one, "Nope."

As bad as it seemed, things just got a whole lot more interesting.

CHAPTER SEVENTEEN

Maya

April 6 2020

This time, when the pebbles hit my window, I know who it is and fly to it, shoving it open. There is Sam, looking cute as ever, wearing a mask. I grin at him and pull on the mask LaRue gave Dad to give to me. Sam stands near the house, next to the window. His eyes are smiling at me, all crinkled up at the edges.

"Love the Mickey Mouse mask," he says.

"Thanks, my neighbor made it."

"I've got bad news." He pulls the mask down so I can see his downturned mouth, then covers it again. "They canceled the prom."

"I'm not really surprised. Things aren't exactly getting better around here, or anywhere, for that matter."

"True, but when this is over," he says, wiggling his eyebrows up and down in a way that makes me laugh. "I'm taking you on a date, and we're gonna dress up nice. Once I get my license, that is. Which is my first order of business when we get released from quarantine."

I'm grinning like a fool beneath my mask. I just love this guy. "I look forward to it. So...did you sneak out again?"

"Yeah, the folks are on their weekly grocery run. I can't stay long, though. They're just doing curbside pick-up." He glances over his shoulder. "Isn't that your dad's truck?"

I look behind him, and sure enough, it is. "I wonder what he's doing home this early?" My mind starts racing with all the reasons Dad might be home. *Did LaRue tell him there was a boy at my window? Did Mom come to him as a spirit and tell him to get home quickly? She would do that.*

"I don't know, but I better run before he comes after me."

I laugh. "Okay, but he's pretty fast, and if you think *I* pack a mean punch ..."

He gives me a wide-eyed look and takes off running as Dad pulls into the driveway.

I honestly don't think my dad will mind. We were talking through masks from several feet away . . . well, a few feet. Of course I'm wrong. Quarantine-Dad is different than regular-Dad. I take off my mask and go into the living room to meet him as he comes in. He is wearing a mask, which is odd, we're in the same bubble—that's what they call the people you live with or hang out with during covid. He stops next to the door, holding his hand out as if I should stay back.

"Who was that?" is the first thing out of his mouth.

"Good to see you too, Daddy," I decide to go with the innocent look to distract him. It doesn't work.

"Boss sent me home. I have a fever, though I feel fine. Who was that?"

"My friend Sam, from school. He just stopped by to tell me our prom was canceled. We were going to go together." I frown with my best cute-puppy face, hoping to soften him.

"Well, I don't want him over here anymore. Don't you understand the meaning of quarantine?"

He is pretty riled up, so I know this is a losing battle. "Okay, Daddy. But, if your boss sent you home with a fever, shouldn't we worry more about you right now?"

"Yes," he agrees. "Look, I'm going to have to quarantine myself in my room until I know what I have. I don't want you coming near me till we're sure it's not the virus. I'll take my meals in there, and everything. The boss says I have to wait two weeks, just to be sure." He doesn't look at me as he says this but busies himself hanging up his coat and baseball cap.

I can tell he's devastated. I feel it then too. He might have the disease that killed Mama and my grandparents. My stomach feels sick, like I might vomit. I take a careful breath through my nose. "Dad, it's going to be okay. I'll bring food to your room. You just rest and get better. You're strong. Even if you have it, you're gonna make it. You'll see." I feel like I am saying this for my own benefit. Fear has taken a grip on my throat.

He glances up at me and his eyes are red-rimmed. He nods and heads past me toward his room. "Can you put some lunch outside my door, honey? And can you check on LaRue? And wear your mask. I sure hope I didn't get her sick."

"Sure, Dad." I hear his footsteps move slowly down the hall, and the door to his room clicks shut.

I collapse onto the floor right where I'd been standing and sob. My dad is sick. I can tell because his eyes are red like he's been crying. I'm sure he's afraid he'll leave me alone. I can't breathe. I wish Mom was here. She'd know what to do.

Chapter Eighteen

LaRue

April 2020

LaRue stirred at a knock on her front door. This was the second day in a row she'd fallen asleep during *Jeopardy*. It wasn't like her. "Probably allergies," she said as she pulled open the door to find little Maya in her mask. There was something wrong with the girl's eyes. They looked tense.

"Hi, LaRue," she said. "Dad wanted me to check on you. Is there anything you need?"

LaRue could tell there was something the girl was not saying. Maya avoided looking her in the eye. "I'm fine, dear. Oh, I see your dad came home early today. Is everything all right?"

Maya twisted back and forth, looking like she wanted to run. Then, as if she'd made a decision, she blurted, "His boss sent him home. He has a fever. He wants me to check on you to see if you needed anything and...how are you feeling?"

LaRue sagged against the door frame. She felt tired. "I'm fine, dear. Nope, don't you worry about me. Your dad will be fine too. He's a big strapping man. You just let him rest and he'll recover fast, you'll see. Don't worry a whit about me. I'm fine."

LaRue watched Maya's eyes relax, and she turned toward her house. "Okay then, let me know if you need anything. I'll tell him you're okay. He was worried he got you sick."

"Give him my love, dear, and tell him I'm just dandy." She closed the door and locked it. *This is not good. What if I got him sick by making him take me in for an X-ray? What if Jonathan has the virus . . . that poor little girl. She cannot lose another parent.* LaRue sank back into her chair and turned off the TV.

What if I really am sick? Is that why I'm so tired? Fatigue was one of the symptoms that everyone mentioned. The thought shot adrenaline through her body, and she sat up straight. She needed to plan. She pushed herself out of the chair with great effort, then went to the small kitchen, pulling a pad and pencil from a drawer and sitting at the round wooden kitchen table.

She'd never really thought about dying, but now it was time. Where was that form the doctor gave her? He'd said to stick it on her refrigerator in case the ambulance ever came. She got up and dug through a few drawers until she found it and got her glasses on to read it. "Oh my, Walter. There are a lot of questions here. I remember when we filled out yours."

She sat back down and read the form: Physician Orders for Life-Sustaining Treatment. Did she want to be ventilated? She sat back in her chair, breathing heavily. "No, I don't think I do." It had been hard watching Walter die—cancer is a hard way to go–but it had never come down to a ventilator. "What did the news say? About four percent of people come off the ventilator alive. I'm not sure I'd want a tube in my throat . . . and then there's a 96-percent chance of dying anyway." She checked no to the ventilator question.

"Do I want to be fed through a tube? No, I don't believe I do." She checked no to the feeding tube question. A couple more checks and it was signed and put up on the refrigerator. "Now I know why it's bright pink. That way, they won't miss it. Smart. Now, what else do I need to do?"

She started a list.

1.   What to do with Hershey? That was a hard one. Would Jackie or Betty take him? Maybe Maya? He was a grumpy old man, but she loved him.

2.   Update the will.

3.   Find all the important papers.

4.

She couldn't think of a number four. Those were the only three things that concerned her. Maybe something else would come to her later, but for now, she'd call her lawyer. She needed to make some changes in her will.

CHAPTER NINETEEN

Ashley

April 2020

Ashley was confused. When she was running in the mornings with Parker, he seemed very attentive and interested. But during these online happy hours, it was hard to read him. Was it just because they were looking at each other through a screen with four other people, or did he have a different persona with his friends than he did with her?

They were online now, and Ashley knew she shouldn't be drinking her wine so fast, but she felt uncomfortable when she'd logged on and been face-to-face with Cassandra.

Cassandra raised a sculptured eyebrow. "Oh, hi, Ashley. I didn't know you'd be joining our group *regularly.*" And then as if to cover. "Of course, any friend of Parker's is a friend of ours." That felt like a slap.

Ashley took the high road. "So how is this quarantine treating you?"

"Oh, marketing has not slowed down at all. We're quite busy. How about you? You're a, what? X-ray tech or something?"

Ashley felt steam building in her head. That witch, she knew she was a nurse. Thankfully, before she could blow, Brandon and Cheryl popped in with happy smiles, followed quickly by Tess. Parker was the last to come on and by then she was stewing over Cassandra's remark, and taking large gulps of wine.

Cheryl started telling funny stories about her morning sickness, which got increasingly hilarious. "Who called it that, anyway?" Cheryl practically shrieked. "It's not morning sickness. It's morning, noon, and night sickness."

Ashley laughed, and thankfully the others laughed too, but *did I laugh too loud?*

Cheryl continued her rampage. "Seriously, I've thrown up in every room of the house. I've even learned which foods go best both ways. Milk is a no, but orange juice is okay."

Ashley laughed so hard wine almost came out of her nose. She may have even snorted. *Did I imagine it, or did Cassandra raise an eyebrow in my direction? Again.* She was starting to hate that eyebrow.

"I'm sorry, Cheryl," she said quickly, trying to stop laughing. "It sounds awful, but it's also so funny."

"Agreed," said Tess. *God bless Tess. She's wiping her eyes just like me.*

Parker was rather quiet, and Ashley was shocked when Cassandra quickly changed the subject away from Cheryl's stories. "Oh, I'm so tired of being confined. I miss being able to go out with you all. Remember the Brewer's Cabinet? I miss meeting up there so much. You were so funny last time we were there, Parker."

Ashley looked at Parker's face. Did it just get pinker? She felt as if they'd just excluded her from the conversation. Why had Cassandra derailed Cheryl's story like that?

Parker took a sip of beer as if stalling for time. "Yeah, those were fun days. I miss them too."

What exactly did he miss? Ashley hated this format where she had to guess at everything. It was different with her work friends. She'd had a similar gathering with them, and it was okay because she already knew them. Here she was the newby, the outsider.

"But you know what I miss most of all?" he asked. "Traveling—being able to get in my car and head over the mountain or get on a plane and fly somewhere. You traveled a lot for your job, didn't you, Ashley? Do you miss it?"

Her body warmed that he seemed to be trying to include her. "I do, in some ways. But it was exhausting too. To be honest, I'm kind of enjoying the break."

His mouth tightened. Did he think she was a stick in the mud that didn't like to go anywhere? She added quickly, "I do miss road trips, though."

"Where do you like to go?" asked Tess.

Ashley felt such fondness for Tess. They were definitely going to be friends in person when this was over. "Oh, anywhere, really. But I love Santa Cruz.

They have the best beaches, and the mountains are nearby."

"I'm in," agreed Tess. "Post-pandemic road trip is on the books."

"Oh Parker," cut in Cassandra. "Remember that road trip we took to Carmel? It was so lovely there."

What the actual fuck is wrong with this woman? Doesn't she understand that Parker is with me? *Is she some kind of feral cat trying to mark her territory?*

Interestingly, Parker ignored this comment. "Road trip to Santa Cruz it is," he said, raising his glass. Ashley let out a breath. *Why are my emotions swinging so wildly?*

After the happy hour, Ashley waited for her phone to ping for her follow-up facetime with Parker. "Well, that was fun," he said as his opening greeting.

"Was it?" she couldn't help the bit of frost that crept into her voice.

"Come on, Ash, you can't let Cassandra get to you. She's just a sore loser, that's all."

"What do you mean? You said you didn't date her."

"Well, not officially, but we went out a few times."

"Seriously? And you didn't happen to mention that to me?" Anger coursed through her. *Am I overreacting? No. Didn't I directly ask him about this before and he said they hadn't dated.*

"Ash, it was nothing. I hate this."

"You hate what?" Fear coursed through her tensing her muscles. *Is he giving up on me already?*

"I hate trying to date you online. I think it's time you let me into your bubble."

"I let you into what?"

"You know, your bubble—people you see in person during the quarantine. We're both staying safe. Don't you think we could be safe together?"

Now she was speechless. He wanted more, not less, of her. "Uh, yeah, sure," she stammered. "So...you want to come over sometime?"

"Yes," he sighed. "I'd love to. How about Wednesday night? I'm beat right now and have meetings all day tomorrow, which always makes my head hurt. But Wednesday night I'll be fresh. Would that work?"

Her chest practically glowed with joy. "Yes, I'd like that. I could make dinner. Do you have any allergies?"

"Not a one." He grinned as he signed off. She was going to have a real, in-person date with the man who made her crazy in more ways than one. Thank God for pandemic bubbles.

CHAPTER TWENTY

Maya

April 10 2020

I gently knock on Dad's door. I don't want to disturb him but, *sheesh,* he's been in there for days. "Are you okay in there, Daddy?"

I know he isn't. I heard him coughing all night. "I've got a thermometer here, so we can take your temperature."

"Just leave it outside the door, pumpkin," he says and coughs some more. Disappointed, I set the thermometer on the floor next to his barely touched breakfast and pick up the dishes. I hate not being able to do anything for him. My own stomach hurts all the time now, like there's a mouse in there tying my intestines in knots.

I dump his uneaten food in the garbage and rinse the dishes in the sink before loading them into the dishwasher and then I scrub my hands. They're beginning to dry out and crack with all the washing. They tell us to sing the *ABCs* when we wash. I never knew that song was so long. I need to find some better lotion. Maybe in Mom's stuff, which of course I can't get to because it's in Dad's room.

Our food supplies are getting low. I open the refrigerator to take stock. We have a little milk, some cheese, and some leftover pizza. How long can I get away with feeding him soup and cheese sandwiches? I check the bread and see that only three slices, including the heel, are left. Dad always did the shopping. I wander into the living room, thinking. *Can I take the car to the store? I don't have a license, and I don't really know how to drive. Plus, I'd have to use his debit card. We're out of cash too. I don't think the store would be okay with that.*

I am so tired. Trying to keep up with online school, take care of dad, and not having enough food, it's all too much. I've rewatched all my favorite shows when I couldn't sleep, and am all caught up on *The Umbrella Academy*. What else am I supposed to do? Plus, I can't see Sam, even through the window, because, what if I'm infected? I walk into the living room and flop down onto the couch, tears welling in my eyes. I try to blink them back. I need to be strong for Dad, there's no one else. I wish Mom was here.

Just then, my phone buzzes. It's Sam. I swipe it open to see his smile, which instantly falls into a frown when he sees me. "Are you okay? What's wrong?"

His kindness pushes me over the brink, and my tears begin to fall before I can stop them. I haven't really told him what's going on. "It's Dad." I sniff when I can get my breath. "He's been home sick for three days, and I think he has the virus." The enormity of that truth, of saying it out loud, squeezes my heart so hard I cannot breathe for a moment.

"Oh no, Maya. I – Dang it, I want to help. This must be so hard for you after your mom, and all. But I can't even get out of my house. My parents are like Nazis. What can I do? What do you need?"

His cute, sad face makes me feel better. I smile at him. "You can't come over, anyway. I don't want you exposed. It'll be okay. It feels better just to have some-one to talk to."

"Well, that I can do," he grins. "Do you want to play a game?"

"What kind of game?"

"It's called '*Tell Me a Story*'. My mom made it up when we used to take road trips to keep my brother and me from fighting."

"Okay." Anything to get my mind off Dad.

"I'll start," he says. "I'll give you a prompt, and you have to tell me a true story about your life. Then you ask me one—and you can't use the same prompt. Okay? Tell me a story about food."

"Food?" That makes me laugh and I search through my food memories. "Well, as you know, we are Italian, on both sides, so food is extremely important. When I was old enough to hold a fork, my Nonno, that's my grandpa, taught me how to swirl my spaghetti on my fork by holding it against my spoon. He told me if I did it without making a mess, he'd give me a quarter."

Sam chuckles. He has a deep chuckle, like it comes from his stomach.

"Hey." I laugh. "I've always been motivated by money. So I worked my butt off to swirl that spaghetti, and I did it."

Sam smiles at me through the phone. "You'll definitely have to teach me how to do that."

"Sure, on our mock prom date we can go out for Italian food."

"Oh, I don't want to embarrass myself in public," he joked. "Maybe I need some at-home training first."

That cracks me up and I tuck my feet up onto the couch to get comfier as he says, "Okay, your turn."

I search my mind for a prompt and feel silly, but this is fun. "Tell me a story about a storm."

"A storm, eh?" He taps his chin with his finger. "Okay, we were visiting relatives in Madison, Wisconsin, and there was this tornado warning. My brother and I whooped and ran outside—stupid Westerners. We really wanted to see the tornado. The wind was intense. It practically blew us over. You should have seen the trees bending way over in the wind. It was fun until my dad came out and dragged us into the house and took us down into the basement where the whole family was gathered. They looked at us like we were crazy."

I laughed. I like getting to know Sam. And it's nice to have something else to think about besides Dad.

I settle back onto the couch. "Sam, can I tell you something I've never told anyone?"

He looks at me with his kind eyes. "Of course."

"And you won't tell anyone?"

He shrugs. "Who would I tell?"

"That's true, I guess." I take a deep breath. "You know when I got in that fight with Jonell on the first day of school?"

"Yep, I remember the blue and purple around your eyes." He grins.

"Well, the thing is, it wasn't *entirely* her fault. I mean, I kind of lied about part of it."

"What do you mean?"

I'm so embarrassed, but I need to tell someone this—it's been eating at me. "I was mad at her for ruining my sleepover. She accused a girl of flirting with her boyfriend, and stomped out, mad, in the middle of the night. We were all having so much fun and she ruined it. So...I put her stuff in my closet and when she texted me to come and get it, I ignored her texts."

Sam looks confused. "That's all, that's the big secret? You ignored her texts?"

"Um, I may have blocked her number too. And one time she came to my house, and I pretended not to be home." My eyes filled with tears. "I mean, what if it's Karma? What if my mom dying and Dad being sick is, you know, payback because I lied?"

Sam shook his head. "Oh Maya." He looked sadder than I'd ever seen him. "I wish I could hold you right now. There is nothing you could have done to cause what is happening right now. Nothing."

I nod, sniffing as tears run down my cheeks. "I guess I know that. It's just so much. Too much, and I've been thinking about everything I've done wrong. Mom and I fought all the time, and she practically took on the whole school board over it, and really, it was partly my fault. I should have told them the truth right at the beginning. But I didn't and it just became this huge thing. And then, before she left, Mom and I had a fight, and I stormed out on her and slammed the door. I can't stop thinking about it. It keeps me up at night."

"Listen..." He looks at me with such loving eyes I can feel it through the phone. "I've told some pretty big lies in my time and had my share of fights with my folks . . . especially with my brother. Those things have nothing to do with this pandemic, Maya. I promise. I'll tell you what. When you can't sleep, you FaceTime me. I don't care what time it is. You call me and I'll stay with you until you sleep. Okay?"

The knots in my stomach loosen a little and I don't feel so alone. I nod. "Thanks, Sam."

CHAPTER TWENTY-ONE

LaRue

April 2020

She was definitely not okay. LaRue sat at the kitchen table, looking at her lunch. "I know I should eat, Walter, but everything is tasteless. It's the darndest thing." She forced a spoon of soup to her lips. Yep, she just could not taste it. What an odd sensation.

At first, she thought something was wrong with the food. She tried a banana. It was awful. Then she tried an orange. Nope, no flavor. And the fatigue wouldn't lift no matter how much she'd slept. But she wasn't coughing and didn't have a fever that she could tell.

What on earth is wrong with me? Am I losing my mind?

She pushed away from her table and realized that Hershey was bawling at her. "What do you want, you lousy cat?"

She walked over to his food. "Looky there, you've got food, and you've got water. What's your problem?" He continued to yell at her as if she was daft. "Hmm, when's the last time I cleaned your cat box?" She honestly couldn't remember, but the smell usually reminded her.

She went to the pantry and bent down, getting dizzy in the process. "What? Oh my. No wonder you're mad at me." The box was over-full. How had she missed the smell? Come to think of it, she still couldn't smell it now, and she knew it had to stink. "I'm sorry, honey. I'll change it right away." She picked up the cat box by the handle on the lid and took it out the back door to the garbage cans. Her ankle was healing nicely, but she still had it wrapped and walked carefully. She'd been dizzy lately, like her blood pressure was funny or something.

"Geez, I wonder if there are other bad smells in the house?" She emptied the box and carried it back in to refill it. Hershey stopped yowling. At least her ears were still working. She went back into the kitchen and looked under the kitchen sink. The garbage can was full too. "I bet that stinks. What the heck is going on?" She carried the full bag out to the trash can and dumped it in. "No wonder I can't eat. I can't smell my food. This is the strangest thing ever."

She went over to the computer in the living room and typed "symptoms of coronavirus" into the search engine. There it was: "Loss of taste or smell." *Yikes.* Just then, the phone rang.

"LaRue, it's Maya. I just wanted to check on you."

"Oh, it's good to hear your voice, dear. How are you? Is your dad feeling any better?"

"No, he's still resting in his room. That's why I wanted to call. I can't get to the store to get your fruit and veggies this week. Will you be okay without them?"

"Oh, of course, dear, don't you worry. I have plenty of food here. How is his appetite? Is he eating okay?"

"Well, no."

"Has he said anything about having trouble smelling his food?"

There was a pause. "No, he hasn't mentioned that. Should I ask him?"

"No, no. I was just wondering. I heard it might be a symptom of the virus. Don't bother him. I'm fine, dear, but thank you for calling. You just worry about him for now."

"Thank you. I'll talk to you later."

LaRue hung up the phone and heard her printer start up. She walked to the living room and saw papers spewing out, it must be a fax. "It looks like Fred made the changes in the will. Now I just have to sign it." She waited until all the pages were out and then took them to the kitchen and stapled them together. She took a deep breath. What seemed like a good idea last week filled her chest with dread today. This could be real. She wasn't the healthiest person she knew, and she was old, at least by the virus statistics—anyone over 60 was "old". If she got it, she could die. Her eyes misted. "Well, Walter, I might be coming along sooner than later I guess." She sat down with a pen and commenced signing.

LaRue got into her PT Cruiser. It had been six weeks since she'd driven, and she was afraid she'd forgotten how. All she'd done is start the car once a week to keep the battery strong. Backing carefully out of the driveway, she pulled onto the road. At least there was no snow to navigate. "Ahh." She smiled. "It's like riding a bike." She had called the covid hotline two days ago, and they said her symptoms warranted testing. She only had to drive a few miles to the Livestock Events Center. She pulled in between the clearly marked lines. Guardsmen and women in uniforms and masks directed her through the maze of lanes that twisted and doubled back like a Disneyland line. Finally, she got up to where cars were stopped in all four lanes. A woman wearing a mask and gloves gestured for her to stop and held up a sign. It said, "Keep your window closed until you get to the nurse, who will test you. Please hold your driver's license up to the window."

LaRue pulled her license from her pocketbook and pressed it to the window. The woman outside leaned close to the window to read it, then leafed through some papers. She seemed to be verifying that LaRue had an appointment. She wrote something on a post-it and taped it to her back window, directing LaRue to move forward into one of the lanes.

Cars filled all the lanes, but things seemed to be moving quickly. There was a long drive to the back of the huge events center building. At the next stop, a man with a mask and gloves approached her vehicle. He took the post-it and dug through a stack of papers until he found the one he was looking for. He held it up to the window. "Please verify your name and birthdate," he said through his mask.

LaRue read the form. "It's all correct." She nodded and gave the thumbs-up sign for good measure. Talking through a mask was hard.

The man handed the form to a guy in a golf cart and told her to follow the cart. "This is surreal," she told Walter. "I feel like I'm in one of those end-of-the-world movies." She pulled the car forward and regretted again that Jonathan had not agreed to come with her. When she called, he insisted he was fine and didn't need a test.

She followed the golf cart to the testing area where the man gave her paper to a nurse who approached the car, looking like an astronaut or a beekeeper in full protective gear.

The nurse told LaRue to roll down her window. "Welcome. Let me tell you how this goes. First, please sign this paper giving us permission to test you for covid-19."

He handed her a piece of paper and a pen, she signed it and tried to hand them back.

"You keep the pen," he said, taking the paper. "Now, take this tissue and blow your nose."

She did as she was told, feeling a bit self-conscious. She'd never purposefully blown her nose in front of someone. It would be rude. The man held out a paper cup, "Please put the tissue in here."

She did so, and the nurse threw the cup in the trashcan next to him.

"Now, I'm going to insert one of these into each nostril," he held up an extra-long Q-tip swab. "It will make you want to cough." She could see that his eyes were smiling and that he looked tired. How many times had he said this today?

"Please cough into your elbow *after* the sample is removed."

The nurse was right, after he stuck the swab way up her nose, she did have to cough, but it wasn't all that bad. The whole thing took less than a half-hour from when she arrived. They said she'd get the results in a couple of days.

"Well, Walter, we wait two more days. I think they got some of my brains on that swab. Maybe they'll be able to tell if I've got Alzheimer's!" She laughed at her own joke and turned toward home.

The streets were so empty that it felt unreal. "It's happened, Walter. The rapture came and I've been left behind."

Chapter Twenty-Two

Maya

April 12, 2020

I'm so scared. Dad is still sick, and we're running really low on food. He asked me to go over and check on LaRue. When I get there, she doesn't come to the door, but I know she's home.

She keeps a key under her mat, so I open the door and stick my head in. "LaRue, are you here?"

I think I hear her voice, but it's too quiet to know what she is saying so I close the door and go look for her. She isn't in the kitchen; I follow Hershey down the hall to her bedroom. I've never been in her bedroom. It's a small room with a queen bed covered in a flowery spread. The door is open and she is lying on the bed looking pale.

I walk up to her bedside. Her eyes are open and blink, much to my relief. "Are you okay?" Hershey jumps right on the bed as if to say "Bug off, human. I've got this."

LaRue nods and tries to speak but her voice is low and raspy. She keeps glancing to her bedside, there's a glass of water there. "You want a drink?" I ask.

She nods. So I try to help her sit up and it takes a while, it's like she is almost dead-weight. Finally, I get her propped up on her pillow and she takes some gulps of water. I wonder how long she's been in this bed. Now she clears her throat, and do you know what she says?

"How are you doing, honey?" She is worried about me!

"I'm okay but how are you?"

"Oh, I'm just having a little trouble getting out of bed."

It's like she just doesn't have any energy at all, she looks like a deflated balloon. "Do you think you have the virus?"

"They called yesterday and said I don't. I just feel muzzy. Like I can't get my breath."

"What should I do? Dad's still sick, and I can't drive."

"I guess we need to call 911."

She says it just like that. I feel so hot. It was like the walls have closed in around me and it's hard to breathe.

She takes my hand. "Look at me, Maya."

I look at her and she squeezes my hand. Maybe I stopped breathing for a minute there and the warmth of her hand makes me start again.

"I have to go to the hospital, but they called yesterday and said I don't have covid. You don't have to worry about me, I'll be fine. But would you take care of Hershey while I'm gone?"

"Of course." I look at the fur pile on the bed. He glares up at me. What do I know about cats? Mom was allergic so we never had a dog or a cat. The closest thing to a pet I ever had was a goldfish.

Then she squeezes my hand again. "You know, you and your dad are the only people I have. You're like a granddaughter to me. I'm very proud of you and I'm praying for you. You'll be okay."

I start to cry then, but she says, "Be strong for me now, will you?"

What can I do? I smile and try to keep my lips from trembling. "I will." Then I take her phone and call 911.

While we wait, LaRue gives me instructions about the cat. "His cat box is in the pantry. There are plenty of cans of his food in there. He only needs one can a day and he'll turn his nose up at it, but don't give in. He'll eat it."

I just keep nodding. My heart pounds as I think about the ambulance coming toward us. I don't want her to leave. She's been the one stable thing in my life these last months when Dad was at work and Mom was gone. She was the one I called when Mom died.

Then we hear the sirens. She gestures to me. "Help me stand up."

I try to help her, but she isn't strong enough, and neither am I. Her knees are shaking, and she sinks back onto the bed. "Well, I'll just stay here then. You go meet them, will you?"

I hug her then. I just pull her in tight and hold her close. She smells a bit sour but still has a hint of the rose-scented perfume she loves.

When I get outside I see it's gotten dark. Flashing lights are coming toward me and the siren is screaming. My heart is in my throat. The firetruck pulls up first, closely followed by the ambulance. Seeing them makes my stomach twist like I might vomit. It makes the whole thing real. The neighbor lady comes out of her place. Ashley, I think is her name. She's the one with the dogs.

"Are you okay?" The poor lady, I don't know her at all, except to see her with her dogs now and then. But she is very kind, and I end up crying all over her as they take LaRue away. When I can talk again I say, "Don't worry, she tested negative for covid. Maybe it's the flu or something."

She nodded but I'm not sure she believed me. "I have to get her cat." My voice is shaking, and my feet feel trapped in cement.

"I'll help," she offers. "Just give me a minute."

We go in and gather the things LaRue told me to. I can't stop shaking. I lock her door and Ashley helps me carry everything home.

Ashley says cats need a few days to get used to a new house, so it's better to leave them in a small place for a while. We decide to lock Hershey in the laundry room with his food and water bowls and cat box. I hope LaRue gets home before I have to take him out of the laundry room.

Dad yells from his room, "What's going on out there?"

"You'd better go," I tell her.

She looks concerned, like she's afraid to leave me.

"I'll be okay, but thanks."

She leaves and I fill Dad in through the door. I can tell he's devastated when he grows quiet. He loves LaRue too. *Now, what will I do? What will I do?*

CHAPTER TWENTY-THREE

Ashley

April 2020

Ashley stood nervously watching out the window as Parker's car pulled into the driveway. It was fun to have a reason to shave her legs, dress up, and put on make-up. In the six weeks of quarantine, she'd gotten lazy with her self-care, that was for sure. After an hour of trying on outfits, she'd settled on leggings and a ruby red cashmere sweater that draped off one shoulder, sexy but not desperate.

Even though she'd been waiting at the door, the knock startled her and sent the dogs barking. She took a breath and opened the door as the dogs rushed out to greet him, happily wagging their tails. They probably thought they'd get a walk since their morning hike was the only time they ever saw Parker.

Wow. He looked fantastic. "You clean up well." She grinned at him.

"Back at you," he said as she stepped aside and he followed her in. He held out two bottles of wine. "Wasn't sure what you were cooking, so I brought a red and a white. I've noticed you like both."

"Salmon..." she said, taking the bottles, "...so the white will be perfect." Her back was stiff, this felt oddly formal. She led him through the living room. "Settle down," she said to the dogs who'd been happily hovering around Parker. They instantly went and lay down on their dog beds in the living room.

"Wow, you've got them well-trained."

She grimaced. She'd had to train them well because Mark had a very low tolerance. "I think they assume you're hiding Princess Jasmine around here somewhere." She placed the red wine on the counter, pulled out a wine opener, and handed it and the bottle of white to Parker.

He took them without a word and opened the bottle while she pulled the salmon out of the oven, the smell of lemon and fish filled the room. It looked perfect. "I guess I should have asked if you like fish."

"I do. That smells amazing." He pulled the cork from the bottle and walked to the small dining table next to the kitchen. Ashley had set it with colorful plates on a brilliant white tablecloth. A single red rose in a white vase graced the table. Parker poured the wine into the crystal wine glasses. "To be honest, Princess was pretty upset that I left. I think this quarantine has spoiled her; I hardly ever leave without her anymore."

"Oh, you could have brought her," Ashley said, putting the fish onto two plates and adding salad sprinkled with strawberries next to the salmon. They were both nervous, she could tell. They spoke so easily on the trail but now that ease was gone.

She straightened the cutlery and he put down the wine bottle gently taking her wrist. "Is it wrong that I wanted you all to myself?"

Her pulse kicked into high gear as he pulled her into a hug speaking softly into her ear. "I've been wanting to do this for so long." He held her there gently. He smelled clean and felt strong against her. He didn't let go until she completely relaxed into him. Then he put his hands on her shoulders and stepped back, gazing into her eyes. "That's better," he said with a smile. And it was.

After the hug, dinner was a success. They talked and laughed, and he helped her clean up the dishes. They moved onto the couch where she served him a small bowl of berries in cream and a snifter of Grand Marnier.

"That was a perfect meal," he said, placing his empty bowl on the coffee table in front of them. "Thank you."

The praise warmed her. It was hard to keep from comparing him to Mark, who always complained about her cooking. Parker's arm was along the top of the couch, and she snuggled closer, resting her head against his shoulder. Was she making an invitation? Yes, she was ready, and he accepted the invitation right away, tilting her chin up and pressing his lips slowly to hers.

The kiss was warm and tasted of berries. It had been a long time since she'd made out with a guy, but she had no other name for what happened next. They were in the middle of a good old make-out session twined together on the couch. She was enjoying every kiss and sensation. The warmth of his body, the weight of it, aroused her. She was about ready to suggest they move to the bedroom.

The sound of sirens split the air. They both sat up abruptly and looked out the window as the sound grew closer. Flashing lights blinded them as first a firetruck and then an ambulance pulled up right out front.

"What's happening?" Parker asked. Ashley wondered if somehow Mark knew what she was up to and called the fire department. He would do something like that just to spite her.

They watched in silence as someone came out of LaRue's house to meet the emergency vehicles. Ashley squinted through the dark and blinding emergency lights to see that it was Maya, the girl from across the street waiving the trucks down.

Dread washed over Ashley. "Oh no. It's LaRue, the one who sews the masks. I'm sorry. I need to go out there." She was already slipping on her shoes and a coat. "I'll be right back. I just have to make sure she's okay."

"I'll go with you," he said, putting on his shoes.

"No, I won't be a minute. Just relax. I'll be right back."

She ran up the sidewalk, stopping near Maya. "What's happening?" she asked. Maya turned to her with a tear-streaked face.

"She's sick. I couldn't get her up. And Dad's sick and can't help her. I can't drive. She told me to call 911. I'm . . . I'm," at that the girl burst into tears and flung herself into Ashley's arms, clinging to her and sobbing.

Ashley felt so sorry for this girl and patted her head. First, her mom and grandparents, then her dad, and now LaRue. She was too young to go through this alone. Just then the front door opened, and they turned to see paramedics bringing LaRue out on a stretcher. Ashley noticed that all the emergency work-ers had on masks, but she and Maya did not. When a fireman came up to them with a clipboard, the girl broke away from Ashley. "They'll be taking her to Renown Emergency," he said. "Either of you related to her?" He waved the clipboard with a bright pink form attached toward them.

Maya leaned in and saw her father's name listed as son. "I'm her granddaughter." She pointed at the form. "My dad and I are the only family she has."

The man handed the clipboard to Maya with a gloved hand. "Please check your name and phone number so we can let the hospital know who to call. I'm afraid you won't be able to visit her, and I recom-mend you quarantine yourself for the next 14 days." He regarded Ashley. "Both of you have now been exposed."

"Oh no. But she tested negative," Maya said.

"When?"

"I -- I don't know exactly."

"Then, consider yourselves exposed, both of you." The fireman took the clipboard back and walked away.

As they watched the ambulance pull away Maya turned to her, "I'm sorry. I snotted all over your beautiful sweater. I'm Maya from across the street."

Ashley smiled and touched the girl's shoulder. "I'm Ashley, and don't be sorry. LaRue's told me about you. You've been through a lot."

Maya nodded, glancing at LaRue's house and back. "She wants me to go in and get her cat but I'm kind of scared. Would you...would you be willing to go in with me?"

It was then that Ashley realized her date was over. Not just her date, but her ability to see Parker in person for at least fourteen days. In that hug with Maya, she'd just possibly exposed herself to the virus, and she couldn't expose him. She needed to send Parker home. Sadness draped her shoulders. "Of course. Just give me a minute. I'll be right back."

CHAPTER TWENTY-FOUR

LaRue

April 2020

"Well, I must say..." LaRue said to the EMT who sat next to her in the ambulance... "in my 75 years, I've never been in an ambulance. It's really rather exciting." They had stuck an oxygen mask on LaRue before she even left the house. She wondered if the EMT could even hear her.

The woman smiled behind her mask and face shield. She had kind eyes. She patted LaRue's hand with her latex-gloved hand. "I'm just going to get you set up with a saline drip. Looks like you might be a little dehydrated."

That made sense to LaRue. Maybe she was just dehydrated. She had a lot of older friends who ended up in the hospital for dehydration. Walter had even been on a drip once; it made all the difference.

The short ride to the hospital went by fast, but when they arrived it didn't feel like the same hospital she'd spent years visiting. Everything was empty, no one bustling around, no people standing in line at the information kiosk or sitting in the waiting room. She'd never seen it like this. All the people she could see were wearing those beekeeper suits. It's the virus, she realized. She had read that no one could visit, and they'd canceled all elective surgeries. This was really weird.

She was placed right into an emergency pod. The EMT squeezed her foot and waved goodbye, and then she was alone. When a nurse did come in, he was dressed in one of those hazmat suits. It was disconcerting. It was like Dustin Hoffman in that movie...what was it called?

"Hello," the nurse said. "I'm Todd. Can you tell me your name and date of birth please?" He moved his stool up to a computer and began typing as she spoke.

She repeated the information she'd given the para-medics. Then he asked, "Have you been exposed to the virus?"

"Well, I don't know, Todd."

Then Todd started rattling off questions he must have asked a thousand times. He didn't even look up from the computer, just kept typing.

"Do you have a fever?"

"No."

"Do you have shortness of breath?"

"Only when I try to get up."

"Have you been in close contact—within six feet—of someone who has covid-19?"

"Well, now. I'm not sure. I went to get my ankle X-rayed a while ago. My neighbor took me. His daughter says he's sick. But he wouldn't go with me to the testing. He's a stubborn one, that boy."

"Was he wearing a mask? Did he cough or sneeze on you?"

Todd was not winning any points with her. It was like trying to talk to a robot. She tried to have compassion. He was probably working long hours and worried about getting the virus himself. "Not that I recall."

The questions kept coming. "Have you traveled recently?"

"No," she said, slightly miffed. "I've been in quarantine with the rest of America."

He didn't seem to notice. "Did a health official tell you that you've come into contact with covid-19?"

"No," she said. "I had the test and they said it's negative."

"Unfortunately..." he said, pulling out some test tubes and sticking labels on them, "... we are finding that 30 percent of our tests produce false negatives, so I'm going to run some blood tests just to rule things out." He swabbed her inner arm, efficiently poked her, and quickly filled several tubes.

"So, what symptoms bring you in today?"

There was the question they usually asked first, but now it was apparently overshadowed by the virus questions.

"I'm having trouble getting up. I just feel very weak and tired lately. Maybe I'm dehydrated." She smiled her best charming old lady smile behind her mask which made her eyes crinkle and worked on most everyone, but didn't seem to be working on Todd.

"Have you noticed any other symptoms?" He said this without looking at her. He was taking her blood pressure and stuck a pulse and oxygen reader on her pointer finger.

"Well," she gave up smiling and tried a little humor. "Everything I eat tastes like so much nothing. Kind of dampens the appetite, you know?"

He took a note but made no response. "Your oxygen level is very low. You rest here and a doctor will be in to see you shortly."

Shortly was a flat-out lie. LaRue lay there for over an hour staring up at a small TV in the corner that showed Judge Judy, but with no sound. The judge eviscerated one plaintiff after another. Hospitals are not nice places. The bleach smells were strong enough to break through her impaired sniffer.

It did not help to have so much time to think; worry started to grip LaRue by the throat. This was no joke. Maya's mother and grandparents died from covid. She could die here. What had her life meant? She had no children–if she'd had children at least they'd be calling her and worrying about her. Besides Maya and Jonathan, no one even knew she was there. She needed to call her friends but didn't know where her phone was.

She had no legacy that she could think of. *Sure, I tried to be kind and loved Walter well. I take food to the sick folks from church and make quilts for the babies. Then there's the food closet. But is that what a life amounts to, in the end, small acts of kindness? Maybe I should have served in the military, or gone to law school to fight for the poor and disenfranchised, or been a teacher at a high-risk school.? I need more time.*

"I'm not ready, Walter. I know it's selfish, but I need to think of something to do, something to contribute. Well, there's Maya. She needs me."

Then, it was as if Walter whispered to her. *Pray, LaRue.*

So. she did, and she began to breathe again. And a peace filled her heart and relaxed her mind. She was not alone here. She was here with Jesus and Walter, and that was enough.

Finally, a doctor came in looking like an astronaut. She had black circles under her dark eyes behind her face shield, but at least she made eye contact.

"Hello dear," the doctor said.

Ah, she knows my trick too, thought LaRue.

"I'm Doctor Patel, and I'll have you moved to a room for the night. We want to check your blood tests. That can take up to 24 hours. Your oxygen is low, but otherwise you look pretty good, so far." The doctor proceeded to listen to her lungs and asked the same set of virus questions. Then she was left alone again until they finally moved her to a room. By then it was too late to call Maya, and she couldn't seem to keep her eyes open. She'd call tomorrow.

CHAPTER TWENTY-FIVE

Ashley

April 2020

Ashley hadn't slept. Thoughts of Parker's disappointed face at being told he had to leave mixed with Maya's grief-stricken expression had kept her tossing and turning all night long. She finally gave up and got out of bed to sip coffee on her couch in the dark. LaRue was in the hospital, unreachable. Maybe that wasn't true. Perhaps she could try to call later and see if she could talk.

And Maya, she would need to go over there and help the girl somehow. She was alone with a sick father.

But what about Parker? He was the best thing that had happened to her in a long time, even better than meeting John because he was local; she got to see him in person. When she came back to the condo to tell him the bad news, he was hard to convince. She rang the bell and stood back from her own front door. He opened it and laughed at her distance, then saw her face. "What happened, what's wrong? Is your friend okay?"

The dogs rushed out to circle her feet. "They've taken LaRue to the hospital, and I can't see you now because I've been exposed to the virus."

"What? How? Did you touch her or something?"

"No, it was Maya, the girl from across the street. She's been helping LaRue and, remember, I told you how her mom and grandparents already died? Well, apparently her dad is sick too. Anyway, she was crying, and I hugged her. I'm sorry. I need to come in and wash my hands. But I've been exposed, so you're going to have to leave."

His face fell. She could tell he understood. He gathered his things and paused a few feet away from her, outside. "I wish I could give you a hug. You look pretty devastated."

"Yes, I am. If it's the virus, I'm worried she won't make it. She's 75, and has arthritis." Ashley sighed. "I was really enjoying our evening. But Parker, this means I can't see you for fourteen days, you know."

He frowned. "Dammit, we were doing so well. But it can't be helped. I'll call you tomorrow, okay?"

"Okay." Ashley held out her arms in a hugging motion. "Long-distance hug."

He laughed and mimed hugging back, then turned to go. She could tell by the way his shoulders drooped that he was as sad about this as she was. "No more quarantine bubble for me. Come on, kids." She snapped her fingers. "Back into the house." The night had ended badly.

Now, she took the last sip of her coffee, which was no longer warm. The dogs, who were familiar with her morning ritual, began to get excited. They thought it was time for their walk. "Okay, gang." She pulled herself off the couch and put her cup in the sink. "We'll go early. Then we won't have to run into Parker.

I don't think I could take seeing him and not being able to run with him."

Ashley knocked on Maya's door after her run and shower, this time she had her mask on. The house was one of the originals for the neighborhood that had become mixed, with condos and small homes over time. She'd always wanted to see inside the lovely Victorian and wondered how much of the surrounding area went with the house when it was built.

Maya peeked out the front window, then opened the door, Ashley almost gasped. Seeing the child in the daylight showed how thin she was, and with the dark circles under her eyes she appeared positively skeletal. "Uh, hi. I'm your neighbor Ashley, from across the street..."

Maya gave a small smile. "I know. Thanks for last night."

It got quiet between them, then Ashley took a breath. "Well, I wanted to see if you needed any help. You said your dad is sick, so, can I go to the store for you or anything?"

Maya glanced behind her, then said softly. "We don't have any cash. I only have Dad's debit card. But I was wondering, do you think LaRue would mind if I borrowed some of her food? She has a lot in that pantry."

"Oh, I'm sure she wouldn't mind. Would you like me to help you get some?"

"Would you?" Maya's smile brightened. "I'll go get some bags." With that, she was gone, leaving the door open.

Ashley leaned in and saw beautiful hardwood floors, a staircase with polished wooden banisters leading up to the top level, and a well-appointed living room with comfortable cream-colored furniture. The wood and the cream furniture with matching cream walls would have appeared barren if not for the large colorful pictures of Italy adorning the walls, huge vases full of silk flowers filled the corners, and accent pillows brightened the couches. Instead, it felt more like a comfy art gallery.

The living room opened onto a long dining area and, beyond that, a large kitchen where Maya rustled around under the sink. The open floor plan made the house seem huge. Maya came back with a paper sack full of other sacks folded in half. She pulled a mask on and followed Ashley across the street.

Maya unlocked the door with a key hanging from a lanyard around her neck. She pushed the door open and stood leaning in, seeming unsure if she should enter. Then she stepped inside.

Ashley walked in behind her and could understand the hesitation. Although it had been less than 24 hours, the house felt abandoned without LaRue in it, even though the small living room was full of her worn recliners, photos, and knickknacks. It was like she was the soul of the house, and now the house was just an empty shell. They stood together in the small entranceway.

Then Ashley took charge. "Give me some of those bags and I'll go see what's in the refrigerator. It will only spoil if she doesn't get back right away. You get the cans and staples from the pantry."

Maya pulled out a stack of bags and handed them to her, then she turned into the pantry and flipped on the light. Ashley went into the kitchen and did the same. She placed the bags on the table next to a green file folder labeled "Last Will and Testament." Seeing it sent a shudder through her. LaRue knew she might not come back. She listened and heard Maya humming as she moved around in the pantry. Ashley opened the file folder and glanced through the stapled stack of papers. Everything is to be left to Maya and Jonathan, *everything.* The house, which was paid for, as was the car, and a surprisingly large bank account, with some other bonds, IRAs, and stocks. This made Ashley smile. At least the child would be cared for if, Heaven-forbid, her dad and LaRue didn't make it.

She opened a paper sack and set it on the counter. The fridge was not empty, but it was not crammed full either. Obviously, only one person lived in this home. She pulled out an almost full half-gallon of milk, some cheese, a half-loaf of wholewheat bread, and some lunch meat. The clear-plastic drawers had a few bags of carrots and some celery, a basket of strawberries and blueberries.

As a nurse, she knew LaRue wouldn't be home for a while, certainly not if she had covid. Older people didn't fare too well with this virus. The thought made her shudder. If she did come home, Ashley would personally get her more food, so why not explore a bit? The freezer was a bit more exciting—two sirloin steaks and a whole chicken. There was ice cream, two half-gallons, and some frozen Twix candy bars. LaRue had a sweet tooth.

Lastly, she dug through the cupboards. LaRue seemed to enjoy Grape Nuts cereal and Cinnamon Pop Tarts. Her three bags were full when Maya poked her head in. "I'm ready, are you?"

Ashley picked up her bags, carried them out to the entranceway, and set them down next to the two Maya had filled. "I'm going to go to the store to get you some better produce, but guess what? There's Rocky Road ice cream and Praline Pecan."

"Oh my gosh," said Maya, licking her lips. "I'm so excited about that. But I feel bad. What if she comes back tomorrow? She won't have any food."

"I'm pretty sure she won't be back tomorrow, but I promise you, if she is, I'll personally go to the store and buy her anything she desires."

"Oh, that's so nice of you. Ashley, you're a sweet person." Maya looked down, "Do you think LaRue will be upset that we did this?"

Ashley smiled knowingly, thinking of the will. "I'm positive that LaRue would want you to take anything you need."

CHAPTER TWENTY-SIX

Maya

April 14, 2020

I'm sitting on the couch, at about 10:00 o'clock in the morning, listening to Dad cough and texting Sam. Someone knocks on the door and I go to answer it, and yes, I look out the window first. I'm not stupid. Anyway, it's my neighbor, Ashley, the one who helped me get the food from LaRue's house yesterday.

I pull open the door, surprised that she would be here again so soon. And she's wearing an intense-looking mask with a blue square on the front, and scrubs, and carrying a bag like a diaper bag, almost.

"Hey," I say.

"Hey." She hands me a paper sack full of produce.

"Thank you!" We stand staring at each other. I don't know if I should invite her in, I mean, I know she came in when we brought Hershey over, and when she helped me bring the groceries in, but does that mean we are in the same bubble now?

"Maya, I'm a nurse and I've come to help your dad."

I can't even tell you how that feels. It's like this cool wave of water just washes over my whole body. Someone is here to help. Tears fill my eyes and I step back from the door.

"I didn't know you were a nurse," I say lamely. The truth is I don't know anything about her other than she is nice and has two dogs.

"Can we sit down a minute?"

So I lead her to the couch and sit at the far end.

"I love your house; it's beautiful."

"Thanks, it was mostly my mom's doing." Of course, my eyes fill up and I try to blink the tears back and swallow the knot in my throat.

"I'm really sorry. LaRue told me about your mom and your grandparents. That's rough."

I just nod. I don't trust myself to speak. My throat feels too tight.

"Anyway, I am a nurse, although I've been working as a training consultant with doctors and nurses in rural clinics for the last two years. I was wondering if you could tell me what you know about your dad's symptoms. Like, how long has he been sick and what medicines he's taking."

I grab my tablet off the couch and pull up the journal to flip back through it. "He got sent home from work on April 6th. Today is the 14th so that's what, eight days?"

"Why did they send him home?"

"He had a fever. He's worried he gave it to LaRue. I know that thought is killing him, even though she said her test was negative."

Ashley nodded. "Do you know if he still has a fever?"

I hear my dad coughing and we both turn and look down the hall. "Well, there's that, it never stops. I don't know about the fever. I gave him a thermometer and all the cold medicines I could find in the house, but he won't let me in. He keeps the door shut and eats a little of whatever I fix for him. Though he did manage to get the ice cream down." That memory made me smile. Ashley smiles too. I can see it in the lines that crinkle around her eyes above the mask. Should I have my mask on? I grab one off the table and put it on.

"How about you? How are you feeling?" she asks.

I haven't really thought about it." I take a quick mental body scan. "I'm tired but I don't feel sick."

I can tell by the lines that crease between her eyebrows she's worried about me. "Don't you have any other family that could be helping right now?"

"My dad has a brother and his family, but they went back to New York to help my grandparents right before the travel ban, so they got stuck there. And LaRue is like an adopted grandma to me but..." I shrug . . . "so, that's about it."

Ashley takes a deep breath and stands. "Would you ask your dad if I can come in?"

I walk her back toward his bedroom door, which is near the laundry room, and we hear LaRue's cat howling. "Is that Hershey?" Ashley asks.

"Yeah, he started doing that this morning. I feed him every day and change his water. I don't know what's wrong. Maybe he's missing LaRue?"

"Has he been out of the laundry room since we put him there?"

"No, I'm kind of scared of him."

She laughs a bit, which I don't think is very nice. "Oh, I'm sure his bark is worse than his bite. And his cat box probably needs to be emptied and cleaned. Do that first and see if he'll come out and let you pet him."

I was really hoping LaRue would be back before I had to do either of those things, but I say, "Okay," as if it is the most natural thing in the world. Then I knock on Dad's door.

"What?" he says in a voice that sounds raspy from coughing.

"Dad, our neighbor Ashley is here to help you. She's a nurse."

"Tell her thanks, but I'm okay."

"I knew he would say that." I whisper. "He's super stubborn."

Ashley leans into my ear. "What is your last name?"

"Hunter."

She steps up to the bedroom door. "Mr. Hunter, I'm here to help and I'm coming in. Are you decent?" She reaches into her bag and pulls out a pair of latex gloves, putting them on as she waits.

It's silent for a minute except for some rustling noises. I guess Dad, who sleeps in his boxers, is pulling on some pajamas or something. "Okay," he says, not sounding too happy.

"Good luck," I say, stepping back. Ashley opens the door, and the sour smell of a locker room washes over us. Then she is gone. I want to stay and press my ear to the door to see if I can hear anything, but that stupid cat keeps yowling.

I open the laundry room door and Hershey is sitting near his cat box looking annoyed. It does smell pungent, and my eyes water. This is the first time he's been out from behind the washer. I bend down and tentatively reach my hand out to pet him. He does not move but presses his cheek against my hand. "Well, look at you." I coo. "You're not such a big bad cat after all." He allows me to give him a thorough rubbing and then I attend to the cat box. *Yuck.*

When I replace the kitty litter, he seems content. Then I have an idea. I shut the door to the laundry room, run upstairs, and close all the upstairs doors. Ours is a big house and I don't want him hiding up there somewhere. Then I open the laundry room door and go to sit on the couch in the living room. Sure enough, a few minutes later he is in my lap. Who knew? I can't wait to tell LaRue. I have tamed her cat.

CHAPTER TWENTY-SEVEN

LaRue

April 2020

LaRue finally got her phone back. When she was admitted to the hospital they took all of her things. Now it was cleaned and disinfected and handed to her with the cord attached to a socket to charge it. She felt excitement rush over her as she pushed number three of her saved numbers and held her breath as it rang.

"Hello."

"Maya, it's LaRue." For some reason tears welled in her eyes and coursed down her cheeks. She hadn't realized how scared and alone she felt until she heard

Maya's voice, and she wasn't disappointed with the greeting she received either.

"LaRue, it's you! Oh my gosh, we've been so worried about you. We called but they wouldn't tell us much. Are you okay? What's happening there? I feel so sad I can't come see you. How are you? When will you be home?"

LaRue chuckled at the girl's rush of words. "Oh honey, slow down. I'm okay. They've got me on oxygen and all my bones hurt, but so far my lungs are clear."

"But what is wrong with you?"

There was pleading in Maya's voice and LaRue wished she had a better answer, but she did not. She'd never been good at lying, but this was one time she'd like to. "Well dear, I tested positive this time for the virus. But they say it's just because I'm old that I have to stay here, and they don't want me to infect anyone else. I'm sure I'll be fine."

The poor child was silent on the line. LaRue guessed she was counting up all of her losses and preparing to add her to the list. "But dear," she marched on, "how is your father?"

"Oh LaRue." Maya sounded relieved to have something else to talk about. "You're never going to believe it. You know the lady who lives next door to you—Ashley?"

"Of course," said LaRue, her spirits lifted just hearing Maya's enthusiasm. Something wonderful must have happened, and that made LaRue feel 100-percent better already.

Maya rattled on. "Well, she's a nurse. I didn't even know that, and she's been coming over and taking care of Dad."

"What? Why, that is a miracle. And he let her?"

Maya laughed. "Oh, the first couple of days were a fight, to be sure, but you should see her. She's amazing. She wouldn't take no for an answer, and he's putting up with her all right. Oh, and I should tell you, I hope you're not mad..."

LaRue heard the uncertainty in Maya's voice. "Honey, nothing you could tell me would make me mad." She smiled at the very thought.

"Well, we were running low on food, and Dad won't leave his room, and I can't drive, so I went to your house and..."

"Oh, dear. I hope you took everything you need."

Maya laughed again and LaRue heard the relief in her voice and joined her. "We did." Maya practically shouted, "I'm so glad you aren't mad. Ashley helped me and she said when you come home, she will personally buy you whatever you need. Oh, it has helped so much. And Ashley has even cooked some for us. I'm not great at cooking and Dad was getting tired of sandwiches and soup. Also, we ate all of your ice cream and I'm loving your Pop Tarts."

LaRue laughed long and hard, which led to a fit of coughing. Maya's worried voice came back over the line. "Are you okay?"

"Maya, I'm better than I've been in a week. Hearing your voice makes me happy and the doctor says coughing is really good for me."

"That's good to know. Dad coughs all the time, so that helps me feel better."

"Now, how is my cranky little boy?"

Maya giggled then. LaRue had not heard Maya sound so happy since her mother died. "He's sitting right here in my lap. I kept him in the laundry room for the first few days, and now he follows me everywhere. I've never had a pet before. It's not so lonely having Hershey around when Ashley is gone and it's just me and Dad."

LaRue felt her heart break a little. Maya was so alone in the world. She pushed away her jealous desire to hold Hershey. "I'm very glad to hear that, Maya. He's a good friend to have in times like these, and I'm sure he is very happy to be with you."

"When can you come home?"

"I'm not sure, dear. They say I have to test negative first, then wait a certain number of days. But the number keeps changing. First, it was two weeks, then it was seven days. I'm not sure they even know. I think they are learning as they go with this virus."

"The news is crazy," Maya adds. "The president said this would all be over in a month. Now people are fighting about if the virus is even real . . . or a hoax! People are so weird. And it does seem like the information about it changes every single day."

"I have to agree with you there. Well, I'm feeling a bit sleepy, and I should get a nap before they come to drain me of blood again. I think this place is secretly run by vampires."

Maya chuckled.

"Will you please give my love to your father, and Ashley too? And give Hershey a squeeze for me. And please stay well, will you?"

"Of course. Ashley has me taking Vitamin C and Zinc, and eating well. She even lets me walk her dogs around the neighborhood to get exercise. She's amazing."

"I'm so glad to hear that. I love you, dear."

"I love you too, Grandma LaRue."

As LaRue clicked off the call she felt her throat tighten and tears slip down her cheeks. *Grandma LaRue.* What would she do without this little family? God knew she needed them and put them right next door. She felt extremely grateful as she drifted off to sleep.

Chapter Twenty-Eight

Ashley

April 2020

Ashley took a deep breath and knocked on the bedroom door. "It's me, Jonathan."

"Come in," he said. It may have been the first time he had not growled at her.

She pushed open the door, noting that it smelled better now. She kept the window open a crack and insisted on changing his bedding and forcing him to take a shower.

"You get in there and get clean or I'm going to wash you right here in this bed," she said. That did it. She hadn't done a lot of patient care in her career, moving quickly into the training position, but she had learned how to deal with reluctant patients during her student rotations. She'd found that she could be just as stubborn as they were.

"You know the drill," she said, from behind her mask. He sat up in bed and muted his TV, which was on a sports program, as usual. He put on a mask, then held out his arm. She placed her bag on the chair next to his bed, pulled out the blood pressure cuff, and wrapped it around his arm. His pressure was good, strong, as always. Then she checked his oxygen level and pulse. Still not great. "Have you been blowing in the spirometer?" She glanced at the tall plastic tube on the table next to his bed. He was supposed to be using it to strengthen his lungs. His face told her he hadn't.

"Look..." she said, "...you have to do this at least five times a day if you want to get better. Your oxygen is still low. If you're going to get back to work and take care of that gorgeous daughter of yours, you need to work with me here."

Jonathan sat back against the headboard. His mouth drooped. He crossed his arms over his chest. Ashley felt an ache in her heart. She sat gently on the bed next to him. "Listen, Jonathan. I know you are hurting with the death of your wife. I get that. But you've got a daughter who needs you. You haven't even laid eyes on her in almost two weeks, and do you know what she looks like?"

"What do you mean?" he grumped.

"I mean she's so skinny a strong wind would knock her over. She's not taking care of herself because she's sad too, and worried to death that you're going to leave her like her mother did."

Tears filled his eyes, and he blinked them back, but she knew this was not the time to go easy on him. "I'm sure it would be easier to give up, but your daughter needs you. Think about what her life would be like if you died too. Who would take care of her?"

He turned his face away from her, his breath shuddering in his chest. She pressed on. "Now, I want you to challenge your lungs five times a day. I'm going to make a chart, and I want you to check off a box every time you use the spirometer. Do you understand?"

He nodded, shrugging like a stubborn toddler.

"And no cheating," she warned and stood up. "Now, assume the position."

He pushed back the covers and stood next to the bed, bending over with his hands on the mattress. She stood over him and pounded on his back, hard.

"Jeez," he said. "If covid doesn't kill me, my nurse will." He tried to straighten, but she pushed him back down.

"You know we have to keep those lungs from gumming up. Now hold still."

"You must have been in the military."

She laughed. "Not hardly."

He panted and coughed. "Well, if nursing doesn't work out for you, I'm sure you'll find a place there."

"Shut up and breathe." Ashley smiled, he was getting snarky, which was better than moping. Hope tickled her spine. Maybe he would recover. She was reading everything she could about how to treat covid. But no one really knew, and she was trying her best to do what seemed most logical.

Jonathan was pretty cooperative as she went through the rest of their routine; her mind wandered to tonight. She would be meeting with Parker and his friends online. She needed to get home and get changed. Between working and helping care for

Jonathan and Maya, she'd been neglecting herself and her dogs. And Parker . . . yes, he was probably feeling neglected too. She hoped to have her own family someday, but if this was the kind of exhaustion that it took to care for two other people, she might want to rethink that.

Ashley's plans for changing her clothes before happy hour didn't pan out. She just didn't have the energy and had passed out on the couch instead. She woke up just in time for the Zoom call and found herself much more interested in her glass of wine than in the coming conversation. *That can't be good.* She was also late to the meeting. She checked herself in the computer camera, straightening her ponytail the best she could, shrugged, and clicked on the Zoom link. Parker, Cassandra, Tess, Brandon, and Cheryl were already chatting when she logged on. She waved weakly as she unmuted her microphone.

"Hey, Ashley," Tess said. "There you are."

"Sorry I'm late. Long day."

"You look like you've been through the wringer," Cassandra chimed, her lower lip protruding in fake sympathy.

Brushing off the blatant insult, Ashley took a breath and smiled. "Yes, I have news. Aside from my job and caring for the neighbors, I've been accepted into the Nurse Practitioner program. I've started taking classes online."

The screen exploded in happy exclamations, but Ashley's gaze was trained on Parker. She'd meant to tell him before this group announcement, but they'd kept missing each other. He looked thoughtful, as if he wasn't sure what to do with the information.

"Well," Parker said, "that *is* news. Can you tell us more about the program? Is it in person?"

"No, it's an online program. The school is in Boston. I'm supposed to go there twice during the two-year program, but who knows about that now that no one can travel? I'm really excited, though. Working with my neighbor has helped me realize that it's not patient care I don't like, it's nursing. I mean, you know, hands-on nursing. But being a nurse practitioner opens the door to a lot of different things."

Tess had her usual wide-open grin. "Doesn't it allow you to prescribe medicine and almost be like a doctor? I mean, I haven't seen a real doctor in years, just our nurse practitioner or a physician's assistant."

"Yep," agreed Ashley. "Without the eight years of school. I'll be taking two classes to start. Pharmacology looks rough. You wouldn't even believe the number of drugs we have to know."

"Sounds like you're going to be busy for a while," noted Parker. This felt like a more profound statement than Ashley was ready to consider at the moment.

"Oh, I'll get in a rhythm soon," she rushed to assure him. "And if I'm symptom-free in another week, I can start running with you again."

"Oh no rush," said Cassandra. "I've stepped in. I'm his running partner now."

Ashley felt her face go numb. Had Parker already replaced her? It had only been a week, for Christ's sake. She didn't even know what to say. She glanced at her image and realized that her mouth was hanging open and snapped it shut. *Yikes!* What did she expect? She was a mess; her hair was pulled back in a sloppy ponytail, and still wearing her dirty scrubs. Her shoulders drooped. *Truthfully, I don't have the energy to give a shit.* The screen was quiet, and she realized that everyone was expecting Parker to fill the space, but he remained silent. Cassandra's face was set in a smirk like a cat who had just gulped down a canary.

"Okay," Cheryl came to the rescue. "My turn for a pregnancy update."

Ashley only half listened. She was still in shock that Parker had replaced her so quickly. She may have laughed out loud when she tried to picture Cassandra in a running outfit. *Was it made of crushed red velvet with sequins on the cuffs? Was she wearing shoes that were completely white because they had never been close to dirt?*

Thankfully the night ended early as Cheryl was too tired to stay on, and the group agreed they'd had enough of Zoom for the day. She sat on her couch and waited for her phone to ping for her after-happy-hour debrief with Parker. Tonight, it would not be fun.

When his face came on the phone, she just stared at him. She'd spent most of the happy hour thinking of scathing things to say to him, and now she was utterly blank. Unfortunately, he was staring too. Finally, he said, "It was hard to hear about your decision to go back to school in front of everyone. Why didn't you tell me?"

"It was hard to hear that you're running with Cassandra in front of everyone too. Why didn't *you* tell *me?*"

He rolled his eyes. She hated eye rolls. Mark was an expert eye-roller. She chewed her lip and waited, determined to wait him out.

After a long, painful silence, he caved. "It doesn't mean anything, Ash. She just suggested joining me since you couldn't. It's no big deal."

"And I suppose she looks great in her jogging outfit." Ashley felt petty as she said it but couldn't help herself. "Can she even run?"

"Actually, she was on the cross-country team in college," Parker crooked his head at her as if in a challenge.

"Of course she was," fumed Ashley.

"Ash, I'm not interested in Cassandra, I told you that. You're the one I'm interested in, but you're not returning my texts, it's like you're ghosting me all of a sudden."

"I return your texts."

"Two hours later."

"That's not fair. We both work, and I get to them as soon as I can. Things have just been a bit hectic lately."

"I know, because of *Jonathan*, right."

Did she hear jealousy in his voice? Was he worried about Jonathan? For some reason, that just made her mad. "Yes, because there is a kind man who just lost his wife, and might be dying, himself." That was a bit of a stretch. She was pretty sure Jonathan was getting better, but she wasn't going to share that right now. "And he has a daughter who is equally lost and needs someone on her side. I'm sorry if that bothers you. And I did try to call you to tell you about my school, but you didn't call me back."

He shook his head. "I didn't get a call." He looked down at his phone, and his picture went away for a minute, when he came back on, he was grimacing. "I did get a call. Damn it Ashley, I was at work, and I totally missed it. I'm sorry. I don't want to fight. Let's start over. Tell me everything. I promise I'll listen. You have my undivided attention."

She breathed a deep lung full of air trying to shake off her anger. "I don't want to fight either. I'm sorry, I'm just so tired." And she began telling him everything.

CHAPTER TWENTY-NINE

Maya

April 21, 2020

I am dreaming I hear a clock ticking. It does not tick consistently, but randomly. And it's getting on my nerves. I wake up and realize it's not a clock but someone tapping on my window. My stomach clenches. It's the middle of the night. I mean, Dad is getting better but he's still sick, and what if it's a robber?

I get up and grab my Mathlete Trophy. Standing to the side of the window I peek out, my heart is thudding so hard I think I might pass out. A man in a hoodie and a mask is under my window. I hold my breath, my knees are shaking, should I call 911? Then he looks up at me and I realize it's Sam. He is tapping on my window. I suck in a breath as I lift open the window. "What are you doing out here?" I whisper.

"I was bored and wanted to see if you want to go for a walk."

"A walk? It's..." I glance at my clock. "...2:00 o'clock . . . in the middle of the night."

"So, do you want to go?" He lowers his mask, smiles like a golden retriever and wiggles his eyebrows, which always makes me laugh. "It's been two weeks and you're not sick so I think we're safe."

I nod and drag the window shut. I pull on my sweats and tennis shoes and sneak out of my room, opening and closing the door as quietly as I can. Chills run up my spine as cool air washes over me. He is standing there in his mask, and I grab mine off a hook by the door.

We walk side by side down the driveway to the sidewalk, breathing through our masks.

"You know, they say that when you're outside it's pretty safe. Do you think we can take these off?" he asks.

"Yes, but maybe we shouldn't touch or anything 'cause . . . you know, Dad is sick, and all."

"Okay."

"Where should we go?" The moon is full and the streets are empty. I've never done anything like this before. Butterflies have started a dance party in my chest. It's like triple excitement with sneaking out, being with Sam, and defying the whole "shelter in place" thing. Can we be arrested for this?

"Let's walk to that little park down the street. Maybe we can swing in the playground." We turn to head that way. The night is chilly, but my sweatpants and sweatshirt are enough. It feels so good to be outside. If it's safe to be outside, I definitely need to get out more.

"Cabin fever is getting to me," he said.

"Me too! It feels amazing to be out of my house right now. Would your folks be mad if they knew you were out here?"

He takes his hands to the sides of his head and pulls them apart as he makes an explosive noise. "Ballistic."

I giggle. He is so much fun. "My dad would have the cops out looking for us in a heartbeat. It's a good thing he doesn't leave his room."

When we get to the park, I notice something I'd completely forgotten. "Uh-oh, no swinging for us." I point to the small playground which is completely marked off with yellow caution tape.

"Oh yeah, I forgot. Parks are closed. Oh well, wanna sit on the back of the park sign? That way if anyone drives by, they won't see us."

We walk to the sign that reads "Wilson Park," scanning the ground beneath it. The streetlight reveals trash and leaves that have blown up against it and icky-looking cobwebs, I freeze in my tracks. "How about we just walk around the park and then head home? I don't want to be gone too long, and walking will keep us warm."

"Sounds good," he looks at me for a long time. "I just wish I could keep you warm."

I feel those butterflies migrating en masse to my lower regions. It is intense, better than anything you see on TV. Like the *thought* of cake can be better than the actual cake. Is this what love in the time of covid is like? Anyway, to break the tension. I smile back and say, "That'd be nice." I start to walk around the perimeter of the park. I wish I could hold his hand and hug and kiss him. I take a shaky breath. "What have you decided about next year?"

"I'm going to TMCC. If it's open. If not, I guess I'll be going there online."

"TMCC, the community college?"

"Yeah. Truckee Meadows."

"I thought you'd go to the university."

"Well, the thing is…" he sounds kind of embarrassed, "…my grades aren't great, so I can't get scholarships or anything. Plus, I don't know what I want to study yet."

"I thought you wanted to be an engineer." I remember him mentioning that once in Science.

"Well, maybe. Or maybe not. But I figure I'll go to TMCC and save a lot of money, get my grades up, and live at home. Then, you know, maybe I'll figure out what I'm interested in. How about you?"

"I was going to go away to a school with a good pre-med program, but now there's no way I'm leaving Dad. I'll go to UNR. That is, that's the plan. You know, I never thought about money when Mom was a doctor. What if we can't afford UNR?"

"Then you'll come to TMCC with me." He links his arm through mine. "I'm not touching your skin, but we can link. I think."

I laugh. It feels good to link. Dad used to hug me every day until he got sick. We walk around the whole park just talking and laughing and then reminding each other to be quiet, and shushing each other, which makes us laugh even harder. It is the best day/night I've had in a long time. When we get back to my house he stops and says, "When will your dad be better?"

"I don't know. Ashley said he's getting better, and he keeps saying he needs to go back to work."

"When your dad is better, I'm going to ask my folks if you can be in my bubble. Then I can come over and we can hang out in the actual daytime. Will you ask your dad?"

The idea makes me happy and totally scared. Why not have Sam in my bubble? His family has been crazy-cautious, and Ashley and I haven't been sick. "Let's give him a week to get on his feet. Then I'll ask."

Sam stops in a dark part of my yard and faces me, taking my hands. "Okay, then will you walk with me tomorrow night?"

I grin, looking at our hands. It's been a while since I've touched anyone except the cat. It's pretty much like Sam and I have been long-distance dating and now we are in person for the first time. "Yes, tomorrow."

Then he leans in, and I know it's going to happen. He's going to kiss me. My mind goes whirring like a computer with too many tabs open: *Should we be kissing? Do I know how to kiss? What if I'm a terrible kisser? But he's going to be in my bubble, right?* Then the next thing I know his lips are on mine, warm and sweet, for just a moment. Then he pulls away, a giant grin on his face and I know mine looks just like his. We've touched, we've kissed, and it's going to be okay.

This is how Sam and I start our nightly "sneak walk." That's what we call them, and since there isn't much to do during the day, I catch up on my sleep with afternoon naps. It is a great week.

Chapter Thirty

LaRue

April 2020

LaRue lay in bed staring at the ceiling. What day was it? How long had she been here? Was it daytime or nighttime? She knew only pain. Every joint in her body felt like it was being crushed in a vise. Was it the virus? Or her arthritis? She didn't know. A tear slid down her cheek. *I want to go home.*

"Walter, I miss you. I wish you were here to talk to. I miss Hershey. I miss my house. I miss my friends. I miss Jonathan and Maya. I'm so lonely, and everything hurts."

Maybe she should press the nurse call button, but she knew they'd probably give her more pain medicine, and she was already constipated. She needed to get up and walk. She needed to eat food that didn't taste like pablum.

"This hospital food is going to be the death of me," she said, then laughed. "I suppose it won't be the food that kills me." Then she remembered that the food at her house had been tasteless as well. It was a symptom of the virus. "At least at home, I knew what I was eating."

Her heart hadn't sunk so low since Walter died. She almost wanted to join him; that would be easier than this endless aloneness. "There's only one thing keeping me here, Walter. I just can't bear to hurt Maya. That child has been through so much already." She took a breath and pushed the nurse's button.

If she took the pain meds at least she could sleep. Sleep, that's what she needed. Just to drift off into oblivion and not think about things she could not change.

CHAPTER THIRTY-ONE

Ashley

April 2020

Ashley knocked on the bedroom door. "It's me, Jonathan. Are you decent?"

"Yeah," came a growl.

That man's attitude was not going to bring her down today. She pushed open the door and was glad to see him sitting up on his bed. The TV was off for a change and he looked slightly human. Had he shaved?

"It's a beautiful sunny day, so get your tennis shoes on."

"What? Why?"

"Obviously your mood does not match the beauty of this day. Now, you told me you want to go to work. That means we have to get you stronger. We are going for a walk."

"Outside?"

"Preferably." She went over to the closet door to look for his shoes. It opened to a large walk-in full of dresses and feminine clothes, and a whoosh of flowery perfume filled the room.

"Shut it," he demanded, his face collapsing into deep lines.

"I'm sorry, I was looking for your shoes." The look on his face was filled with such anguish that she thought she might cry. Crying would not help him. She knew he was missing his wife, but he had a daughter to think about. She put her hands on her hips. "Well, where are your shoes?"

He pointed weakly to another door that opened to a much smaller closet where she found a pair of battered tennis shoes that looked like they belonged in a landfill. She held them up as if she'd found a dead mouse in the closet. "Are these all you have?"

"Yes, I use them to work in the yard."

"Socks?"

He got off the bed and shuffled over to a dresser. "I'll get them. Don't need you rifling through my underwear."

"Especially if your underwear looks like these shoes." She knew how to dish it; she had a brother. Did he just stifle a smile?

He sat on the bed and took a very long time to put his shoes on.

She huffed. "Are you trying to get on my last nerve? Do you want me to do it for you?"

He did not answer, just glared at her, and worked faster.

"Now, before we go, there is something I want you to see." She walked past him and pulled open the curtains which had a view of his lush backyard.

He held his hand to his eyes squinting at the bright daylight. There was Maya, her back to them, throwing a ball for the dogs and laughing at their antics as they chased it.

He sat silently watching her, his head cocked to the side. He said, as if to himself. Then, "It's Sophia," as if he remembered Ashley's presence. "My wife was about that age when I met her . . . only a few years older. She took my breath away. Maya looks just like her." He sat silently as if lost in thought, then barked, "Whose dogs are those anyway?"

"They're mine. Pepper is the black one—lab and border collie mix. Westly is Weimaraner-ish, the brown one."

He sat as if transfixed. She watched his face move through several emotions. He looked mad, as if he was afraid the dogs would poop in his yard. Then he looked sad, and then wistful. "She never got to have a dog."

"Oh?" was all she could think to say.

"Sophia was allergic to dogs and cats. It's too bad. Every kid should have a pet. A goldfish just doesn't cut it, you know?"

"I agree. Now she has LaRue's cat, Hershey, and she's been great at helping me with the dogs. She's been taking them on walks around the neighborhood for me. They've been a bit neglected lately."

As he watched his daughter his face softened. "I miss her," he said so softly she almost didn't hear.

She wondered if he meant Maya or Sophia.

"You ready?"

He slowly pushed himself off the bed. "Do I need a sweatshirt?"

"Probably." She opened the door. "Today we will see if we can get down to the stop sign and back. We'll increase it every day until you're strong and can consider going back to work."

"Aye-Aye captain." He gave her a mocking salute.

She smiled leading the way to the front door where the coats hung on a Victorian coat rack. She much preferred his snarky attitude to his melancholy defeat. There was hope for him yet.

CHAPTER THIRTY-TWO

Maya

April 28, 2020

Ashley has to study for her first test and asks if I'd be willing to walk my dad today. The request sounds like "Will you walk the dog today?" It makes me laugh but, of course I agree. I am excited and nervous. It's been over two weeks since I've even seen him. I knock on his door, wearing my mask.

"Dad?"

"Yeah?"

"I'm your walking partner today."

He opens the door holding his T-shirt over his mouth and nose. His wrinkles look deeper, and his clothes hang on him, he's lost so much weight. There are dark circles under his eyes. I try not to let the shock show in my face.

"Did Ashley say it's okay?"

"Yes. I'll meet you at the front door." I wait by the door until he is ready to go. Once we get outside, I take off my mask and blink at the sunshine. "Ashley says when we are outside we don't have to wear them."

He peels his off too. "Thank God; these things are hot."

We start walking in the cool air and I am following his lead, Ashley has been taking him and I don't know the drill. "How far today?"

"Let's see. Yesterday we did four blocks so today we add tw——six blocks. That woman is a tyrant."

I laugh at that, Dad is not used to taking orders from women. Except Mom. I'd seen her persuade my dad to her will over and over, but I doubt he even knew it was happening.

"What are you laughing at?" He turns to me with a pretend frown.

"Oh Dad, I'm so happy you're getting better. I was really worried. If Ashley is helping you then I'm glad she's hard on you. Have you heard anything else from LaRue?"

"When I call, they always say she's sleeping. They don't really give me updates."

"Me neither."

Dad's not walking fast but he isn't walking so slow that I have to slow down. He seems pretty strong. "Dad, I have some things I've been wanting to talk to you about."

"Okay." He looks at me with a raised eyebrow.

"Well, school is almost out, and I don't know if I should register for UNR or TMCC?"

"TMCC? Why would you go to a community college? You're going to med school."

"It's just that I didn't know, now that Mom's . . . gone" I take a breath, I've never talked to my parents about money—it's a touchy subject. "Do we still have the money for college?"

He stops then and turns to look at me. "Pumpkin, your mom and I set up a college account the week you were born. You've got nothing to worry about."

Relief washes over me; we continue walking. He goes on. "I still wish you'd consider going to a better school."

"Nope. I'm not leaving you. And UNR is a great school. I've been researching it, and they even have a good Med School, if I decide to stay here. Don't even think of trying to talk me out of it. Besides, who knows, we may not even get to go to classes. The whole thing might be online. And you know the drill, I'll be going all over the place for my advanced training, so I might as well do the first four here."

"I know the drill," he agrees. "I've got to admit, I'm glad you'll be home for a while longer. I already felt terrible that you're missing your senior year, and then I go and get sick. I'm sorry; it's been rough on you."

This makes my eyes water for some reason. I guess it feels good that he knows a little of what I'm going through. The next question is scarier for me to ask. "Dad, you know Sam? The guy who was supposed to take me to prom?"

"That boy I saw outside your window that day I came home early?"

He does not sound happy. What would he say if he knew we'd been sneak-walking at 2:00 a.m. for the last week? I am certainly not going to tell him, but I decide to rip off the Band-Aid and get this over with before I lose my nerve. "Yes, well, he's my boyfriend, Dad. And his family has been fanatic about social distancing. And, once we're sure you're well, I'd like you to get to know him. I'd like him to be part of our bubble so he can come over and visit."

He stops again and turns to look at me. "Your boyfriend? How old are you again?"

"Dad! I'm almost 17. Old enough to learn to drive. And he's 17, though he doesn't have his license because his test got canceled by the pandemic."

He is quiet for a long time then starts walking. I wish I could hear what he's thinking. I lose track of how many blocks we've gone but I don't want the walk to end. It feels so good to be with my dad, and I know not to interrupt his thoughts. I look at the houses we pass, the manicured lawns. People on bicycles pass by and wave at us. It seems like a lot of people are out and about. I guess everyone has cabin fever.

Finally, he says, "I guess I'd better meet this guy. But you know that school is top priority. No boy is going to derail your education."

He sounds like his old self, and I can't even be mad. "I know, Dad. Sam is going to college too. I'm determined to be a doctor like Mom. You don't have to worry."

He shakes his head. "I've been a mess, Baby, and I'm sorry. I just kept thinking—wishing— your mom was going to come back and make everything better. I thought it had to be a mistake. And when she didn't come home, I just felt mad at her . . . and every*thing,* and every*body.* But I'm sorry I haven't been paying attention to you. It's time to get my head out of my ass. Oops, sorry."

I laugh then, long and hard. It's not like I've never heard my dad swear but it feels good, and normal. "Dad, Ashley said there are these stages of grief, the denial one, like thinking Mom is coming home. I feel that too. Every morning I expect to see her and then I have to remind myself she's not here."

"Ashley says that, does she? Is she a therapist now too?"

I push him with my shoulder, knocking him slightly sideways. "She's done a lot for me, Dad. You should be nicer to her. Do you know that she's been buying us groceries and helping me cook our meals? She is teaching me to cook."

"I didn't know that, but the meals have been better. Wait, she's been buying us groceries? Do I owe her money?"

"No, she helped me use your debit card to get a Walmart account set up. We plan the meals and order the groceries online. Then she goes up to the store and they bring them right to the car."

"You're using my card, eh? What else have you been buying? Do I need to check my balance?" He grins sideways at me.

"Nothing. But now that you mention it . . . I could use some new shorts. It's warming up, and I'm getting taller. My shorts are like Daisy Dukes."

"Then, by all means, get yourself some shorts. They need to go at least to your knees."

That makes me laugh.

"That's four blocks," he says. "We can turn around here and it will be eight. *Ha!* I'll show the tyrant.

Ashley said I have to go on a hike when I've reached eight. She says hiking will help my lungs because there will be hills to climb. It's the next phase in my recovery. But she's been bad-mouthing my tennis shoes." He stops and points down at his shoes. "They look fine to me."

I look down and, let me tell you, they do not look fine to me. "Dad, they look like they've been chewed on by Ashley's dogs."

"Well, do you think they'll let you order tennis shoes on that Walmart site?"

"We can find some on Amazon. I'll help you when we get home." I put my arm through his as we turn back. It is such a good day. I feel like I could fly home. Dad is getting better.

LaRue

April 2020

"Is that you Walter?" LaRue spoke into the dark room. "I'm ready, if it's time."

Ashley

April 2020

Ashley stared at her computer in disbelief. Her boss stared back at her, looking like he'd just eaten a lemon. "I'm sorry Ashley, someone had to go, and you were the last hired. You've done a great job, but there's just not enough work for everyone now that we can't travel."

She knew it was true, she'd seen John Chen struggling to keep his clinics open with covid taking all the medical resources. No elective surgeries were being done and there was no time for preventative health. Her job involved helping small rural clinics with wellness training, but now that that had all been put on hold to deal with the virus, all traveling had stopped. She loved her job. "Is there a chance that maybe . . . I'll be hired back on later?" She hated to sound desperate.

"It's hard to say. No one knows how long this will go. The president says it will be over in May, but the scientists tell us this is just the beginning. I'd pick up another job if I were you. You'll get a great reference from us, of course. I hear they are desperate for traveling nurses in New York."

She nodded, trying not to cry. She had to stay professional. "Well, thank you, Bob. You've been great to work for. Perhaps in the future, we can work together again."

"I hope so. I'll email the termination documents today."

"Okay."

There was an awkward pause where they just stared at each other. Then he shrugged and glanced at his watch. "Well, I have a meeting. Goodbye, Ashley."

"Goodbye." The screen went blank. Now she let her tears fall. She was in shock. Her job was her proudest achievement. It allowed her to start paying off her condo when Mark left and kept her free to sign up for graduate school. She'd made a lot of money as a training consultant. In two weeks all that would be gone.

Part of her wondered about her termination. Yes, she was the last hired but she knew she was better at the job than the other employees. Family comes first, she guessed. It was a family-run company and when push came to shove, they protected their own. That thought sat like lead in her stomach.

She would have to apply for unemployment right away, along with half the country. Pepper crawled up on the couch; she was the one most sensitive to Ashley's feelings. As soon as Ashley put her computer on the coffee table, Pepper put her head in Ashley's lap. "What'll we do, girl?"

Of course, as a nurse, she could get a job anywhere right now. And Bob was right, traveling nurses make tons of money. But to throw herself into the fiery pit of covid... She'd seen the videos of New York; the place was a mess. They had portable morgues in parking lots. *What would I do with the dogs? Who would take care of Maya and Jonathan, and LaRue when - if she came back?* She sighed as Pepper licked her face.

Could she afford to keep her condo on unemployment? *Maybe I could downsize into a smaller place and rent this one out for a while. Or possibly move in with Parker?* She knew it was early in their relationship but …

Her brain was circling the *what-ifs* when her phone beeped. She lifted it, glad to see Parker's face.

"Hi." He grinned at her, then his grin fell. "What's wrong? Are you okay?"

"I just got laid off." She hated to say it out loud. That made it true.

"Oh no, what happened? Not enough work for you now that no one is focused on preventive health?"

"You got it."

"I'm sorry, Ash. That's awful. What will you do?"

"I don't know, nursing? Travel nursing maybe; they need lots of nurses in New York."

"New York, you can't go there. It's a hotspot."

"I know." She felt the breath leave her like a deflated balloon.

"Can you afford to stay in your place?"

"I doubt it." She moaned, then gave him the opening. "I might have to rent it out and find something smaller for a while." She waited, holding her breath.

He was quiet for a moment as if considering. "Well, I'm sure you'll figure it out. Are you still helping Jonathan?"

"Yes." Her shoulders drooped. He was not going to suggest she move in with him. "Why do you ask?"

"Well, it's just that it's been a couple of weeks, but I realize now that every day you're over there it pushes our reunion back two more weeks."

"Oh." She knew that was not exactly true but chose to ignore it.

"And, if you start nursing in a hospital, then..."

He didn't finish the sentence. What was he saying? "Then?" she prompted.

"I can't be exposed, Ash. I have to stay well to help my folks."

"Okay. So what are you saying?"

"I'm thinking we should just take a break. It's not like we've even really started dating. We had one date that was, you know, interrupted. Maybe you can call me when you've decided what to do with your life."

"What?"

"It's probably for the best, Ash. We can't see each other now, and we don't know when we will be able to. If you start working as a nurse it could be months."

Suspicion filled her, she felt her eyes narrow. "Are you saying that because you want to date Cassandra?"

"Ash." He reacted strongly, perhaps too strongly. "No, it just makes no sense to be exclusive when I can't even see you."

"Oh, okay. So, you want options. Just tell me, is Cassandra on the list of options?"

"I'm not even going to dignify that with a response. I'm going to go now before I get mad. Call me when you know you're off the untouchable list." He hung up.

His words were seared into her brain like a tattoo. "The untouchable list?!" He wasn't willing to wait for her. He wanted someone to touch. Well, Cassandra was definitely on the touchable list. She knew it in her knower, she'd been dumped for the girl with the snakelike eyebrows.

She sunk onto the couch to text Maya. "I'm taking the day off. Can you please walk your dad today, and maybe take the dogs this afternoon?" She pushed send and then laid down on the couch, curling next to her dog. She would not move from this position today, she was sure of that.

CHAPTER THIRTY-FIVE

Maya

May 4th, 2020

Dad let Sam into my bubble! The doctor told Dad that he had to be symptom-free for five days and then he could go back to work. He starts again Monday. And Sam has been allowed to come over.

Today we are all on a celebratory hike up Evan's Canyon. Sam and I are out in front with Westly and Pepper circling us. Dad and Ashley are bringing up the rear. The sun is out and I can't stop smiling.

Dad is determined to do the whole two-mile loop. The weather is weird, like it always is during May in Reno. It rained yesterday, but today is perfect and the sweet smell of sagebrush after the rain fills the air. I love that smell.

Sam and I are goofing around when I hear Dad yell, "Maya." The tone of his voice is scary, like he stepped on a rattlesnake or something—they start coming out when the weather warms up. My heart jumps right up into my ears as I turn to race back, with Sam close behind. When I get to them, he has his phone to his ear.

"It's about LaRue," he says. "I'm waiting for the doctor to come to the phone." His face is creased in worry. I instantly grab his free hand. We both need support for this phone call. I try to still my breathing. Ashley is grimacing and Sam is fidgeting from foot-to-foot. The dogs chase each other around us in happy circles, unaware of our dread.

Then Dad's head jerks up and pushes the button so his phone goes on speaker, then turns up the speaker so we can all hear. The doctor's voice comes over the phone.

"This is Doctor Patel. I'm LaRue's doctor here at Renown. Is this her son?"

"Yes," Dad says without hesitation. He might as well be.

"I'm calling to let you know that LaRue has made a dramatic recovery over the last few days."

"Oh." Dad's shoulders come down from his ears and I let go of my breath as we all take in the good news. I see Ashley swipe at a tear. "That's fantastic," Dad says, "To be honest, we were bracing ourselves for the worst."

"Well, it was touch-and-go for a while, given her advanced age, but she is one strong cookie."

That makes us all laugh. True statement.

"I'm calling," Doctor Patel says, "to give you the good news. I don't get to make that call often on our senior covid patients. Now let me hand you to our social worker, Jason, to give you the details of her release."

"Thank you, Doctor. Thank you so much," Dad breathes.

"Thank you," we all echo as the phone makes sounds of being passed.

"Hello, this is Jason Simmons, LaRue's social worker."

"Hello," says Dad.

"The good news, as Dr. Patel said, is that your mother will be coming home early next week if she continues to improve. The problem is that she won't be able to live alone for some time, until she gets her strength back. It could take a while, even some months. So, I need to find out what you want to do. She tells me she lives alone. A nurse could come in, but she will need 24-hour-care. She's weak and that makes her a 'fall risk'. Or we could move her to a rehabilitation hospital or an assisted living-type facility. Or," he hesitated before saying it, "depending on your situation, might she be able to stay with you?

"She can absolutely stay with us," Dad says and my heart swells with love for him.

Relief washes over me. Thinking of LaRue in an assisted living facility, when they are locked down by the virus, and we wouldn't even be allowed to visit, is awful. People are dying like flies in those places.

"Great, I'll call you the day before she's released and tell you when you can come to collect her."

"Thank you," says Dad, and the call is disconnected.

We all look at each other and then Sam, Ashley, and I start hooting and jumping around while Dad grins and shakes his head at us. The dogs bark as if in celebration.

"Thing is…" Dad says when we all settle down, "…she's going to need a first-floor room."

He lets that sit in the air between us. The master bedroom and my bedroom are the only two on the first floor, the rest are upstairs. I know what he is asking. I only hesitate because living upstairs would mean no more sneak walks with Sam. Sam's been bringing a blanket and we've been exploring more than the park. But, with Dad getting well enough to leave his room now, and with LaRue moving in, the sneak walks will be over anyway. Besides, Sam is in my bubble now and I can see him during the day. I must admit I'll miss those walks in the dark. They were really romantic.

"She can absolutely have my room," I say, echoing his enthusiasm. "I can move upstairs. It'll be fun to redecorate. We can bring over her furniture and make her room feel just like home."

"I'll help you decorate," says Ashley. "I love to paint."

"I can help with the heavy lifting," adds Sam.

"Great," agrees Dad. Between all of us we can get it done by next week. "But that leaves you, Maya, to be the person to keep an eye on LaRue, because I'll be going back to work. That's probably not how you envisioned spending your summer vacation."

That is harder to think about. *We don't know what condition LaRue is coming home in. Can she eat, or will I need to mash up her food and feed her like a baby? What if she needs help showering, or I have to change her diaper?* My throat gags at the idea.

"I can help," volunteers Ashley as if she's read my mind.

Relief floods me. "It's okay, Dad." I swat at Westly whose cold nose is sniffing my legs. "I'm stuck at home anyway, and having LaRue there will make it more fun." I try to smile convincingly.

He grins around at all of us. His eyes are a bit glossy, and he nods, swallowing hard. "Good," is all he says.

CHAPTER THIRTY-SIX

Ashley

May 2020

Ashley was stretching up to roll Butter Up-yellow paint onto the wall of Maya's new upstairs bedroom. The former upstairs guest room furniture had been taken to the garage and Maya's furniture piled in the middle of the room under a drop cloth. Maya wanted a cheery room to lighten up this dark time.

"It's going to look great," said Ashley. "I feel like I'm in the middle of a lemon meringue pie."

Maya laughed. "When Dad puts in the white accent molding it will look even better. Dad said I could order some cobalt blue accent pillows and a matching blue comforter."

"I love me some accent pillows." Ashley wiped at her face leaving a smudge of yellow by her nose. "When we get this second coat finished, should we start moving LaRue's stuff over to your old room? That way this can have a chance to dry."

"You want me to text Sam? He said he would help move stuff."

"Sure." Ashley dipped her roller into the paint and rolled it in the pan a few times to spread the paint evenly, then turned back to her wall.

"You haven't said much about Parker lately," said Maya.

Ashley froze mid-stroke. "Well – there hasn't been much to say. He doesn't want to see me since I'm continuing to be exposed to the virus."

"What? But you can see him now. Dad is all better."

"The thing is, I lost my job, and I might have to go back to work as a nurse, so I'll keep getting exposed."

"Lost your job *and* your boyfriend? Now that's a bad week. I'm sorry Ashley," Maya put her hand on Ashley's arm.

"Tell me about it. I should be applying already but I just can't bring myself to do it. Traveling nurses make great money but, do I really want to leave you and LaRue and go to New York? What would I do with my dogs?"

Maya plopped down cross-legged onto the floor. "We could keep the dogs, but I'd be sad to see you go."

"I'd be sad to go. And now that I'm in grad school I don't know how to do both classwork and extra-hard covid nursing work. The nurses there are all pulling extra shifts. When the hospital called about LaRue, I thought about moving into her house to help her, then I could rent out my place, but your dad offered to bring her here so quickly. I'm not sure what to do, but I need to make a decision soon." Ashley stood back and inspected the wall. "There, how does it look?"

"It looks great. Is my side okay?"

Ashley walked around the room. "Fantastic, how about a lunch break? Leftover pizza?"

"Perfect!" agreed Maya jumping to her feet.

Ashley pushed her decisions to the back burner again. It was easier than facing them.

CHAPTER THIRTY-SEVEN

LaRue

May 2020

"Oh Walter, you're not going to believe this. I get to go home. I get to go home. I'm so excited. Well, not home exactly, but to Jonathan and Maya's house. I can't wait to see Hershey. I wasn't sure I was going to make it and, to be honest, I wasn't really sad about that. I wanted to be with you, Walter, but I also wanted to be with them. I guess God's not finished with me yet. Oh, I've got to call 'the girls' and tell them I'm going home."

After signing a pile of papers, LaRue sat on her bed waiting. The nurse had gathered her things into a plastic bag with a drawstring top. It now sat next to her on the bed. She had grown impatient when an orderly knocked on her door. The strikingly handsome young man came in, pushing a wheelchair. His nametag read Javier. "Are you ready to go, milady?" He bowed with a flourish. "Your chariot awaits."

She could tell he was grinning under his mask as his brown eyes seemed to sparkle. She grinned back. "Yes, my prince, I am."

He helped her off the bed and into the wheelchair. She was surprised at how weak she felt, her muscles shaking in the brief movement from bed to chair. It took a moment to catch her breath. He settled her bag of belongings onto her lap, lowered the footrests, gently placing each foot on a footplate, and finally wheeled her out of her hospital room. "We have a surprise for you," he said with a hint of mystery.

Before she could ask what he meant, they entered the last hallway to the exit. Shock hit her like a tidal wave. The hallway was lined with doctors, nurses, and hospital staff, all clapping. Balloons were tied to the front desk, and some held signs saying, "You did it." and "Congratulations, LaRue!"

Her hand flew to her mask and tears flowed down her cheeks.

They stood in their protective safety equipment and clapped, giving her thumbs-up signs, and waving. She recovered enough to return the love by blowing kisses and saying, "Thank you" over and over. She knew why they were doing this. Not many old people walked away from the hospital after the virus. It was a mixed blessing, to see their joy and relief, but it only underlined the dark circles below their eyes and the deep worry lines on their faces. They were warriors, heroes, on the front lines of the battle. She would never forget them, never.

As Javier rolled her out the front door she blinked at the brightness of the day. Then she saw a grinning Jonathan standing next to his wife's Volvo. Maya stood next to him holding a bouquet of yellow roses. He looked thin but his straight back told her he was going to be fine. Maya looked older; she had grown up these last weeks. The tears began to fall again. Her mask was getting soggy. Jonathan opened the front passenger door and helped her move into the car while Javier steadied the wheelchair from behind, then bowed with a smile before heading back into the hospital.

Jonathan secured her seatbelt as if she were a child. *Oh, how the roles reverse for the aged,* she thought.

"We are so glad to see you." He kissed her wet cheek.

Maya placed the roses on her lap and whispered, "Welcome home."

LaRue could barely speak as they drove the short distance home.

But Maya prattled on the whole way home. "We moved my bedroom upstairs and put you in my old room. Ashley helped me paint and I can't wait for you to see it. And Hershey will be so glad to see you."

"I feel so embarrassed that you have to take me in after all you've been through," LaRue said when Maya took a breath.

"Nope," Jonathan said with finality, "I don't want to hear that. You are our family now and you belong with us. We are very glad to have you, and you can stay as long as you need. Forever, if you want."

Her throat closed up then. Boy, was she emotional, or what?

When they pulled up to their street, she saw her little home, looking lonely and forlorn, but when Jonathan pulled into the driveway of his large Victorian, another surprise met her. A hand-lettered sign over the front door read "Welcome Home, LaRue," and happy pink balloons danced in the breeze around it. Ashley stood ready, grinning and waving as she pushed a wheelchair out toward the car.

How thoughtful of them. "Where'd you get that?" she asked as Maya opened her door and took her roses.

"A place called 'Community Chest.' Ashley found it for us."

Ashley arrived. She looked different somehow too. Less carefree? *I'll need to ask for the story behind that look. The virus changes everyone.*

Ashley set the brakes on the wheelchair next to the car. "Welcome home, LaRue." Then she was all business. "Now swing your legs out and take my hands and I'll help you stand."

LaRue had never felt so well-managed in her life. She'd always been strong and independent, suddenly Ashley was picking up her feet and putting them on the wheelchair footrests. She wasn't sure how she felt about it all. But she had no time to think about it now. Jonathan relieved Ashley as the wheelchair driver and deftly got her up the two steps into the house. He stepped inside and turned her around. The three faced her now.

"You're home," said Jonathan. "What is your pleasure? Food? Couch? Bed? You name it, you can have it."

She looked at their eager faces. "I'm so glad to be out of the hospital. And I'd love to visit, but suddenly I'm very tired. Might I see my room?"

"Of course," Jonathan said, and Maya led the way, Ashley following behind the wheelchair like a parade. He stopped at the room across from the kitchen and turned into it.

Another shock. "Oh my," she gasped. "It's my room; you brought my room over." Tears threatened again, and then she saw the most welcome sight of all. Hershey lay, plop in the middle of her bed, looking at her with the sweetest grumpy face ever. "Hershey," she breathed.

She looked around at the three happy faces that now circled her. "Thank you. Thank you all so much."

Chapter Thirty-Eight

Maya

May 10, 2020

I couldn't sleep that night after Ashley told me all she was going through. Finally, I came up with a plan. The only problem is how to get Dad on board. So tonight, when he came home from work, I had made a great dinner—steak, baked potatoes, and corn on the cob—his favorites.

I set the table like Mom used to do for special occasions, using the good china and cloth napkins. I even lit candles. You can bet he knows something is up. His eyes widen as he comes in, puts down his stuff, and sits at the table.

"I just wanted to surprise you," I say innocently when he raises an eyebrow at me.

"Where's LaRue?"

"She decided to eat in her room again."

"You're not trying to butter me up to tell me you're skipping college to run off with that boy, are you?"

"That boy's name is Sam and, no, I told you already, that's not going to happen. There is something I want to talk to you about, but let's eat first."

He looks at me with squinted eyes, but when I jump up and bring out the food, he can't resist. It's so good to see that his appetite is back. He practically licks his plate.

"How was work?" I venture when he takes a breath.

"Boss still has me on the desk, but next week I'll go back out in the field."

"That's good."

He wipes his mouth with his napkin, sits back in his chair and stares at me, waiting.

"Dad, did you know that Ashley and her boyfriend broke up?" I want to work up to this slowly, so I started by trying to make Dad feel sorry for her.

"I didn't know she had a boyfriend."

"Oh." That is a surprise. As much time as he and Ashley spent together, I assumed he'd know. "Did you guys ever talk about anything?"

He looks at the ceiling as if he was searching his memory. "Well, she mostly yelled at me like a drill sergeant, and I did what she said. Sometimes we'd talk about your mom."

That takes my breath away. Dad doesn't talk to me about Mom, but he talks to Ashley? Well, I guess I'm glad he is talking to someone. I had no idea he'd be so clueless about Ashley's life, though, since they were together every day.

"That's not even the worst thing." I soldier on. "She also lost her job. And now she's thinking of going to New York as a traveling nurse."

The sides of his mouth turn down at that, a good sign. "Why would she want to go there? The virus is terrible there."

"She had a great job, Dad. She loved what she did, and she made a lot of money, but she was the last hired so she was the first to be let go when covid hit. Now she can't afford to keep her place. She'll need to sell it and move, or maybe downsize to an apartment and rent it out, and she might have to quit grad school."

"She's in grad school?" He looks genuinely confused.

What does he think—that Ashley just hangs around with us because she's independently wealthy? "She just started. It's online. She wants to be a nurse practitioner. But now, if she has to go to New York, she won't have time for homework."

He shakes his head. "I can't believe she never mentioned any of that."

"Well, Dad, you have been a little, um, preoccupied lately."

His eyebrows meet in the middle, is he mad? Then he shakes his head again, "You're right, I guess. I feel like I've had blinders on since your mom died. Then getting sick. I couldn't see anything but my own problems."

Now is my chance, he is ready, so I speak fast without taking a breath. "Dad, I have an idea I think might help all of us. If Ashley moves into the upstairs office, she can help me with LaRue, and she won't have to pay rent because she'd be keeping an eye on me and helping LaRue. Maybe she can help with cooking and shopping for food. And, then you wouldn't have to worry about us being home alone when you're working. Then Ashley can get renters so she can keep her place and she'll have time to do her schoolwork." Then I suck in some air and wait.

So many emotions are flitting across his face. It's like he's having a whole conversation that I'm not a part of. He purses his lips. "I don't know, honey, that woman is a bit much. It would be like living with Hitler."

That cracked me up. "She wouldn't be Hitler to you anymore, Dad, 'cause she wouldn't be taking care of you, only me and LaRue, and you'd be working."

"I would relax if I knew you weren't here alone with LaRue. I wouldn't mind her keeping an eye on you with that boy around. I'll think about it."

I clench my jaw so I won't say anything about Sam. This is no time to argue. "You will? That's great."

"Hey, hold your horses. I said I'll think about it. That's all. And don't say anything to her. We need to get LaRue settled. That's enough to think about right now."

I clamp down on my excitement. He didn't say no, and that is practically a yes when it comes to my dad. I can't wait.

CHAPTER THIRTY-NINE

LaRue

May 2020

LaRue sat on the edge of her bed looking at her walker. She should get up and do something, but it felt as if a vitality vampire had snuck in during the night and sucked out all of her energy. Her cell phone beeped, and she leaned back on the bed so she could reach it from her nightstand without getting up.

"Hi, hon. It's Betty."

"Betty, how are you?" Hearing her friend's voice normally cheered LaRue but now it just seemed like one more thing to drain her.

"I'm doing well, staying in mostly."

LaRue heard Betty's oxygen tank in the background. Her friend had COPD and that kept her tied to oxygen on bad days. "Bad-air day?" She tried to smile as she said it.

"A little, but I'm calling to check on you. How is your recovery going?"

"Well, to be honest, it's slow. I'm frustrated, Betty." LaRue pulled her legs back up onto the bed and propped herself against her pillow. Hershey glared at her for disturbing his rest. "I thought I'd be up and running around by now, but I feel like a wrung-out dishrag."

"What does the doctor say?"

"I have a follow-up today. 'Nurse Ashley' is taking me. Frankly, he'll probably say it's normal and I just need to give it time. I'm sick of hearing that."

"Well, you know what they say, we just don't bounce back like we used to. The older we get the longer it takes to recover."

LaRue felt bad for complaining to Betty. She would get better, eventually, but Betty would have COPD forever. "That's true."

"Listen," said Betty. "I don't want to keep you from resting, I just wanted you to know I'm thinking about you, and when you get stronger, Jackie and I want you to come over and have coffee on the porch. They say it's safest outside, and we can sit six feet apart."

"Oh, that would be lovely," LaRue said with as much enthusiasm as she could muster. "Give Jackie my love, and I'll keep you posted. Stay well."

"Alrighty now. Talk to you soon." The line went dead and LaRue let her hand drop from her ear to the bed. Maybe she'd just stay in bed a bit longer.

There was a tap at the door. "LaRue, you up yet?" It was Ashley. The annoying woman insisted that LaRue get up and do her exercises every day. Well, today she could just stuff it.

"No, I'm staying in bed today. Go away." To her chagrin, the door opened a crack and Ashley stuck her face in.

"Aren't we the grumpy bear today?"

"Don't infantilize me," LaRue groused.

Annoyingly, Ashley came into the room and sat on the bed next to LaRue. "There is something I want to talk to you about."

"I'm tired." LaRue turned her head toward her pillow hoping Ashley would take the hint and leave.

"LaRue, I read that one of the symptoms of covid-19 can be depression. I think that might be what you are experiencing."

Now LaRue was really annoyed. "Depression? Just because I'm tired and it's taking longer for me to get my energy back doesn't mean I'm depressed, Mrs. Freud. Have you seen me crying in my beer?" LaRue didn't mention that she had been crying more than usual but she kept those tears to her middle-of-the-night wakefulness.

"Well, my friend." Ashley placed her hand on LaRue's arm. "Depression doesn't always look like sadness. It can look like fatigue, which you have for sure, and it can look like... grumpiness."

LaRue barked, "Grumpiness? You'd be grumpy too if people were always interrupting your sleep. Now get out of my room. Can't a person have any privacy around here? As soon as I'm strong enough I'm moving home where I can rest in peace."

"Okay," said Ashley. "I'll let you sleep until we go to the doctor at 10:00, but we'll be discussing this with him."

"Humph."

Ashley stood up and LaRue heard her open the door and then say under her breath, "No, you're not grumpy at all. You make Hershey look like Little Mister Sunshine." Then the door closed.

It was the first time in a week that LaRue had smiled.

The doctor, a handsome fellow with warm brown eyes that LaRue had always liked, was annoying her. He'd been listening to her heart for a good five minutes. "Dr. Brown, has my heart gone missing?"

Ashley, who was sitting on the chair next to the examination table, rolled her eyes.

Dr. Brown took the stethoscope from his ears and stood up. "LaRue, I'm just trying to make sure your heart and lungs are okay. Covid-19 can weaken them, but I think I'm satisfied that yours are still strong. I'd like to check back with you in a month."

"Ha!" said LaRue, turning to glare at Ashley in victory. "I told you I was fine."

Ashley pursed her lips, frown lines creasing her brow.

"You'd better watch out, missy," barked LaRue, "or your face will get stuck like that."

"Ladies," interrupted the doctor with a wry smile. "Is there anything else you'd like to discuss today?"

"Nope," said LaRue at the same time Ashley said, "Yes."

There was a stare-down between the two until LaRue looked down at her toes hanging off the table. "She thinks I'm depressed."

"And what do *you* think?" asked the doctor.

LaRue shrugged. She knew she was acting like a child, but she couldn't seem to help it.

"Well, have you been sleeping more, or less, than usual?" asked the doctor.

"More," admitted LaRue.

"How has your appetite been?"

"I haven't been very hungry lately."

"How about the things you normally enjoy, have you been doing them?"

"Like what? I'm stuck in someone else's house with a nurse that won't leave me alone, and I can barely walk. What exactly would I be up to?"

LaRue did not miss the look that passed between the doctor and Ashley. She crossed her arms over her chest in protest.

"LaRue," the doctor put his hand on her shoulder and gently squeezed. It felt warm through her thin cotton blouse. "It is not uncommon to become depressed after a major illness. It has nothing to do with you as a person. It doesn't mean you are weak. It's the body's response to a huge assault. It often happens after a big surgery as well. Do you remember Walter getting depressed after his cancer surgery?"

LaRue looked up, nodding.

"Did he take the anti-depressants I prescribed?

She shook her head, frowning. "No, he did not. I did try to get him to, and he refused, the stubborn old mule." LaRue did not look at Ashley, she was sure the girl would be rolling her eyes again. Was she going to be as stubborn as Walter? He'd been a pain in the ass for months after that surgery. She'd felt desperate to help him, but he refused to even try. Eventually, the depression passed but the cancer came back.

"Okay." She didn't want to put anyone through what she went through with Walter. "I'll try them."

Dr. Brown continued to stand in front of her. "You'll need to promise me you'll try them for at least two weeks. Sometimes it takes a while for them to work. Stopping early will not help you. Can you agree to that?"

"How long will I have to take them for?"

"It's not a life sentence. We'll check in on you every few months to see how you are doing. When you're back to 100-percent, even 80, we can titrate you off. You can't just go off cold-turkey though, okay?"

"Okay," she agreed. *What harm will it do, really? No one needs to know.*

CHAPTER FORTY

Ashley

May 2020

Ashley placed silverware next to the dishes on the table while LaRue, in her wheelchair, which was pulled up to the end of the table, cut tomatoes for a salad. Maya was in the kitchen, which opened to the dining area. She pulled a steaming homemade lasagna from the oven. The aroma of bubbling cheese and marinara sauce filled Ashley's nose and her stomach growled. Embarrassed, she glanced at LaRue.

LaRue laughed. "We'd better eat soon, or that tiger in your tummy might devour you."

Ashley giggled.

Jonathan came out of his bedroom. Ashley noted that he looked all cleaned up from work. He scanned the room. "That smells amazing. You three have outdone yourselves, what's the occasion?"

Ashley brushed back a curl that had escaped her ponytail. "Lots to celebrate today. Maya just had the last class of her entire high school career, for one thing."

Jonathan stepped into the kitchen where Maya had just slid a pan of French bread onto a tray and closed the oven door. He pulled her into a hug. "Good job, honey. You did it, and this year has not been easy. I'm proud of you. Are you ready to graduate?"

She smiled up at him and stepped back. "All ready. Sam and I have been decorating our mortarboards for this weekend's party."

"So, let me get this straight," Jonathan said. "We drive through the school at 10:00 o'clock, and they give you a diploma?"

Maya laughed. "Well, that's what they said. I'm not sure what it will be like. I thought we could maybe decorate the truck and sit in the back so we can see everyone."

Jonathan turned to LaRue. "Do you think you can get up into the truck?"

"Of course," she replied. "I wouldn't miss it for the world. I'll just need a boost or a step stool."

The timer rang and Maya pushed her dad out of the kitchen as she opened the oven, checked the bread, closed the oven, and reset the timer. The smell of garlic joined the other fragrances, and Ashley's stomach growled again. "Sorry," she said to LaRue. "I forgot to eat lunch."

"Girly..." LaRue brandished her knife in Ashley's direction, "I don't think I've ever forgotten to eat a meal once in my life. You need brain food for all that studying you're doing."

"We're ready, everyone," Maya announced. Ashley scooped the remains of LaRue's salad cuttings into her hand and threw them in the kitchen trash. Maya pulled the bread from the oven, and Jonathan carried the lasagna to the table. Maya cut the bread, and Ashley brought over a bottle of wine she had opened earlier to allow it to breathe.

They all sat, and Jonathan poured wine in their glasses, then lifted his in a toast. "To Maya. Even though this has been a year of great personal loss, and a global pandemic, you graduated with a 4.2 GPA. Well done."

They all called out, "To Maya!" and sipped their wine.

"Should you be drinking that, Maya?" asked LaRue.

"Ah," Jonathan answered for his daughter. "She's Italian—been drinking wine since she sucked it from a bottle as a babe."

Maya laughed, put her hand up as if to exclude her father, and said in a stage whisper, "Please don't let Dad know I don't really like it."

Jonathan shook his head as if disappointed. "Now, what else are we celebrating? What did I miss?"

Ashley cut the lasagna into squares and began serving. "You had your first day back in the field."

"That's right," he agreed. "And let me tell you, I'm sore already. Who knew my muscles would atrophy so fast?"

There was laughter around the table. The bread and salad were passed as Ashley added, "And LaRue started using a walker today with her physical therapist."

Maya grinned broadly. "That's fantastic!"

LaRue made a dismissive noise. "Oh, that's nothing. I could have done it last week if that therapist wasn't such a bully. He's making me do all these strengthening exercises and will only let me do so much at a time."

Jonathan waved his fork at Ashley, who suddenly found her lasagna very interesting. "I know exactly what that's like." She ignored the gibe.

They enjoyed the food, chatting about this and that until all were full, and when Maya stood to pick up her plate, her dad motioned for her to sit down. "Since we're all here, I was wondering if we could have a family meeting."

Ashley wasn't sure what that meant. "Should I leave?" She started to stand.

"No," Jonathan said. "You're family. This concerns all of us."

Ashley watched his face; he didn't seem mad or anything, what could he want?

"I'd like to make a proposal to you, Ashley, and to you too, LaRue." He looked at each of them. "And it's open to discussion for all of us, although it was Maya's idea, so I know she's on board."

Ashley turned to Maya, who grinned back at her like she had a secret, then she looked at LaRue who gave her an "I have no idea" shrug.

Jonathan turned to Ashley. "Maya has told me about you losing your job and applying to be a traveling nurse in New York, and also about your graduate school. I -- *we* wanted to see if you might reconsider. I could use your help here with Maya and LaRue since I'm back at work. You could either sell your place or rent it out and live here to save money. Then, you wouldn't have to go to work while you study. Unfortunately, I can't really pay you, but I can feed and house you if you'll help with my ladies?"

Ashley mulled over his words. She'd already applied for the job in New York and received an offer but had not signed a contract. She was excited about her graduate program and didn't want to stop her classes now. But, to let go of her place, to move in here, to be, what? A nursemaid, a babysitter?

LaRue jumped in. "Just how long do you think I'm going to be here, Jonathan?"

"Well, I don't know the answer to that," he admitted. "But the truth is you're still very weak. You're sleeping a lot; Maya says most days you're only up for a couple of hours. I don't want you living alone until you're much stronger."

"Oh fiddlesticks," LaRue said, but she didn't argue. Ashley knew Jonathan was right. LaRue wasn't bouncing back quickly. She could easily picture a long recovery. The doctor said covid patients often had weakened hearts or compromised lungs as side effects of the virus. Was that happening to LaRue?

"Just hear me out," he continued. "I'm proposing nine months-to-a-year, for Maya to get through her first year of college, for Ashley to get through one year of graduate school without working, and for LaRue to get stronger. What do you think?"

The table was quiet while Ashley considered the idea. She would love to stay and not have to work while she finished school. She could probably get through even faster if she didn't have a job . . . but to let go of her place?

LaRue spoke first. "Well, if I get better sooner I'm going home." She glared around the table. "You know, I had a lot of time in that hospital to think, and I've decided I might want to start dating."

Maya's mouth fell open. Jonathan's eyes grew wide. Ashley covered her lips with her napkin to keep from laughing. Of all the things LaRue might say, no one had expected that.

"Oh, don't look at me like that. I'm only 75. I could have another twenty years. And I don't think Walter would mind. Once I get stronger, I'm gonna have Maya help me set up one of those online dating profiles."

Ashley could see Maya was also trying not to laugh but gamely joined in. Maya said, "I'd love to help you, Grandma. We'll get you dressed up in different outfits and do a photoshoot."

"Perfect." LaRue grinned. "And another thing, if Ashley is going to take care of me, then I'm going to pay her. I have long-term health insurance, and I bet they will pay for that. If not, I have savings and a pension. You'll get paid for your work, girl. I'll make sure of that."

Ashley smiled. She liked the thought of getting some pay out of the deal. The rent might pay her mortgage, but she had other expenses. "What about my dogs?" she asked.

"They can stay here," Maya blurted, which warmed Ashley's heart.

The dogs seemed to be a balm to the child. Giving her a reason to get out of the house and play with them. Dogs were used in therapy for a reason, just petting animals released endorphins in the brain.

"So," Ashley pondered aloud, "I'd stay where? Upstairs?"

"Yes," agreed Jonathan. "There is a study up there with its own half-bath. You'd have to share the shower with Maya though. Sophia used the room as an office." Ashley noticed he choked a bit on the words, but he took a breath and kept going, "We can convert it easily into a bedroom. In fact, we can do what we did with LaRue if you want . . . bring your whole bedroom right over."

The idea was starting to warm in Ashley. "And, with the cost of rents skyrocketing, I could rent out my place for a year for enough to pay the mortgage plus a little extra. Then I'd get to study. What exactly would be my responsibilities here?"

Jonathan looked at Maya. "You'd keep an eye on this scamp, help LaRue, and maybe help with picking up the groceries. We can all take turns cooking and we can all help keep the house up."

Ashley decided it was a perfect offer. She'd been hoping for something to keep her here . . . and it would only be for a year. She nodded. "I think that would be great."

"Yes," said Maya, jumping up and down in her chair.

"There's only one other thing," said Jonathan, a stern crease between his eyebrows and his fork waving at her. "You'll be here for Maya and LaRue. You will *not* be here to boss me."

Ashley pressed her lips together, but her shoulders shook anyway, and LaRue snickered until Jonathan's fork turned her way. "And you, I don't need any bossing from you either, and no politics."

"But surely you can't still trust the 'orange menace'."

"We don't talk about it," he said.

Now all three women were grinning, and giggles were escaping from Maya, who interjected, "What about me, Dad? Can I boss you?"

His head tilted to the side as if considering. "Well, maybe once a week, if you have to."

They were all laughing, and Jonathan was shaking his head. "Why did I ever agree to this? *Three* women in my house? I must be a masochist."

CHAPTER FORTY-ONE

Maya

May 30, 2020

I haven't been able to sleep for days. The image of George Floyd being suffocated by that policeman while his fellow officers stand by haunts me. I decided I had to do something, but what? Dad wouldn't let me go to the memorial, so I didn't ask him.

Dad's been letting Sam and me take walks, so it was no trouble leaving the house for the George Floyd Memorial, but I don't tell Dad that's where we're going. We live only seven blocks from where the memorial is held so we head downtown with a lot of others.

The crowd is subdued, with everyone wearing masks, and keeping their distance. Some hold signs that say things like "I can't breathe!" and "Mama!"

I can't stop my tears. The video of this grown man on the ground, the policeman kneeling on his throat, is seared into my eyes. Sam walks very close to me and holds my hand. We are both scared because it could turn violent, but it's important to be here.

I've never been afraid of the police before, but I had a black friend once who told me how her parents coached her on what to do if she ever got pulled over. They said to keep your hands on the steering wheel so the police wouldn't have cause to shoot her. I can't even comprehend living like that. It hurts my heart. The stories keep coming out about unarmed black people getting shot, kids even. What is wrong with our world?

Sam and I hold hands walking to the plaza. It is very quiet and respectful. There are a lot of police along the way, just watching. And at the plaza there are some songs of mourning, a few speakers, and then we have nine minutes of silence, the amount of time it took George Floyd to die with a policeman's knee on his neck, while the other policemen stood by and watched. Nine minutes, which felt like forever.

Chapter Forty-Two

Maya

June 11, 2020

Graduation is bittersweet. It's fun when Sam and I don our caps and gowns. We jump into the back of Dad's decorated truck and drive around the school waving at everyone. Sam's parents are in the car behind us honking and waving the whole time. Even on the way to the school, people on the road honk and wave at us. Ashley put balloons and crepe paper streamers in our school colors all over the truck.

Still, it feels empty somehow, not to be able to hang with my friends, although truthfully, I don't have any friends but Shannon, who I've kept in touch with since the pandemic. We've all drifted apart . . . even Shannon has been MIA. But Sam still has a few friends left. If life were normal, we'd be taking lots of pictures, and I could at least say goodbye to my teachers.

So, the best part is the party waiting for us when we get back to the house. Dad takes us inside and makes us stand there looking at the closed curtains that cover the sliding glass door to the backyard. Sam and I giggle like kids while we wait for the cue to come out. Dad said when we hear the music, it's our cue. My heart is pounding, like it's a wedding, which makes the whole thing slightly awkward. I glance at Sam, wondering if he feels it too, but he just grins at me and raises his eyebrows, breaking the tension.

Then we hear it. "Pomp and Circumstance." Classic Dad. Sam opens the curtains and slides open the door then gestures for me to go first. I walk out slowly to the beat of the music, so I can take it all in. There are balloons, a table with a big cake, and a buffet of food. Dad and Ashley are sitting on one side of the yard in white plastic chairs. LaRue is next to them in her wheelchair. Sam's folks are on the other side with his older brother, who is home from Oregon State for the summer. Everyone is wearing masks, but I can tell they are all grinning. We march right up to the middle of the lawn, and everyone is cheering. Then we grab our caps and throw them into the air!

They all jump to their feet to congratulate us. "Can I see your caps?" asks Ashley as she picks them up off the lawn. "Whose is this one?"

"Mine," I say and step closer. "See, it says, '2020-You can't defeat me'."

Her eyes twinkle up at me as if remembering every-thing we've been through in the last months. "Good one, and true. I love all the sequins." She hands it back to me and then looks at Sam's cap.

"It's from Lord of the Rings," he explains. "'Go where you must go, and hope.' Gandalf said it."

"I love it," says Ashley, handing it back. "We need hope right now."

"Come see your cake," says Sam's mom, who is standing near us. We walk up to the table. Somehow, they have gotten a picture of us together, probably off Sam's phone, and put it on the cake with "Happy Graduation 2020" written across the top.

"How fun," I say, getting my phone out to start snapping pics of my own. It may not be the graduation party we wanted, but I am glad to have Sam and his family here with us. Who else would I have invited anyway? But I do miss Mom. And my aunt and uncle and their kids. They are still in New York with my grandparents. They would have come if covid hadn't changed the world.

I feel a hand on my shoulder. It's my dad. "Thinking of her, pumpkin?" he asks. He can always read my face.

"Yeah. Thanks for the party, Dad, it's great. I was just thinking about who might have been here without covid changing everything."

His eyes are glistening, and he holds up his phone. My grandparents from New York smile up at me from their couch. "Happy graduation," they shout. That makes me smile. I get to talk to them, my aunt and uncle, and my precious cousins. It helps me a lot. I have to wipe a tear when they all sign off.

LaRue calls me over to her wheelchair. She'd taken off her cloth mask to put on her portable oxygen mask. Today has probably been hard on her. "I'm so proud of you." She smiles up at me like I'm her own granddaughter. "I put a little something for you in here." She hands me a card. "I loved the parade. But I'm wondering if you'll get Ashley for me, dear. I think I need a nap."

"Of course, but don't you want something to eat first?"

"Save some for me."

"Okay." I glance at the table. "That won't be hard. There's enough food for the whole school."

I walk back to the buffet table and find Ashley dishing up food and I tell her what Grandma said. She looks down at the plate. "I was just making her up a plate. Do you want it?" She holds it out to me.

"Sure." I take it, adding a few more things. There's sliced ham and potato salad, and my favorite salad—ambrosia—which I pile on, plus tons of snacky things, then join Sam on the porch swing, which is shaded by our big old cottonwood tree. "What a day."

"Did you get any good presents?" he asks.

"I haven't looked at any of them yet. Grandma LaRue gave me this card."

"Open it."

So, I put my plate on my lap and rip open the card. A check for $500 falls out. "Five-hundred dollars," I whisper. I've never seen that much money.

"What? That's awesome," he says. "What will you buy?"

"The card says, 'For school clothes, supplies, and textbooks.' Wow. Just wow." I search for LaRue, but she's gone. "I'll thank her later. I can buy clothes, but I wonder if anyone will ever see them?"

"Seriously, will they open the classes?" Sam digs into his food.

"I don't know. Maybe the labs, but I'm sure they'll do the big lectures online." I stare at the check in awe, my mind racing with possibilities.

"Guess what my dad gave me for graduation." Sam's eyes gleam.

"What?" I pop a chunk of pineapple dripping with whipped cream into my mouth and happiness fills my stomach.

"He got me an appointment for a driver's test on the first day they're open. I'm not even sure how he did it. He must have been up, on the computer, at midnight, when the dates opened up. You know what I'm going to do the first day I get my license?"

"What?"

"I'm going to take you on a real date. Even if we can't leave the car to go into a restaurant. Maybe a picnic somewhere in the mountains. I don't know, but it will be epic."

I laugh and lean my head on his shoulder. Sam is a great boyfriend. He's always thinking of things we could do together.

"Did Ashley get moved in yet?" he asks.

"Not yet. We got the room cleaned out for her. That was kind of hard, boxing up Mom's books and things. But maybe I'll be able to use them when I get to medical school. This week, we'll move Ashley's stuff over, and put the rest in the garage. She's already got a *For Rent* sign up. I think it's going to work out."

"Who knew how much our lives would change?" There's just a little melancholy in his voice as we finish our lunch. Then in typical Sam fashion, he jumps up. "Let's cut the cake, I want to eat your face."

After LaRue is tucked away in bed and Ashley and Sam and his family have gone home, I crawl onto the couch with Dad. He sips whiskey; I sip hot chocolate. The evening has cooled off, and we have a fire in the fireplace.

"Did you have a good day?" he asks.

"The best." I say, meaning it. "Of course, it would have been better if Mom was here, but it was the best it could be in these circumstances—a Corona-Virus graduation."

"You know, a lot of the guys at work don't believe the coronavirus is real."

"What?" Disbelief floods me with anger. I sit up, staring at him. "How can they say that after everything you went through? . . . After we lost Mom and Nonna and Nonno?"

"It's weird." He shakes his head. "They believe me, but they think the numbers released by the CDC aren't real virus deaths, like it's some kind of conspiracy—like the doctors are listing other deaths as covid deaths to get more money from the government." He shrugs. "The country is getting really odd. Half of them aren't wearing masks like it's a violation of their human rights. And they rag on me for wearing mine. I just don't get it."

"It is demoralizing."

"Wow, already talking like a college student, are we?" He taps my arm.

"Well, it's true. First, the pandemic, then the race riots, and now everyone is shouting conspiracy theories. I don't even want to go on social media anymore."

"Agreed," he says. "I'm not going to watch the news much anymore."

I know that is a big one for Dad. He loves to watch the news.

"Dad, I didn't tell you at the time, but Sam and I went down to the Black Lives Matter protest."

Dad just about jumps off the couch. "You did what? I saw that on the news, Maya, there were people breaking windows at City Hall. You could have been hurt. And what about the virus risk?"

"It wasn't like that when we went, Dad. It was a peaceful demonstration, and everyone was wearing masks and keeping their distance. It was after we left that things got bad. I think it was people who came in from out of town to cause trouble. If trouble had started, we would've left in a hurry."

He glared at me, so I pressed on. "I had to go, Dad. You saw what they did to George Floyd. When is this going to stop?"

He shook his head again, sitting back on the couch. "I don't know about you, kid. You remind me of your mother, more and more. But, please, promise me you'll tell me if you do something like that again. I can go with you; in case it goes south. Some of the cities are getting violent."

It isn't hard to make that promise. I'd love to have Dad with me if I go again. It was kind of scary, even with Sam there. I change the subject and don't mention that I went to the George Floyd candlelight vigil too. "I did hear an interesting phrase the other day though." I take a sip of my chocolate and liquid happiness warms my throat, "'corona-coaster.' Like, every day is different, some days you wake up and feel good, some days you wake up and you feel down, like on a roller-coaster—but it's a 'corona-coaster'. That really describes it for me."

"Me too," he says. Then he puts his arm around me and squeezes my shoulder. "Well, honey, if we have to be on this corona-coaster, I'm glad we're on it together."

"Me too, Dad. Dad, do you think it's gonna work? You know, having Ashley and LaRue here and everything?"

"Well, I think we can make it work. What did Sam's cap say, 'You do your best and hope?'"

"Something like that, Dad. Something like that."

Chapter Forty-Three

Ashley

June 2020

Ashley was sitting on the bed in her new room folding clothes when Maya poked her head in the door. "Can we talk for a minute? I need some advice."

Ashley's eyes widened. The girl was very independent, keeping her own counsel. If Ashley's door was open, Maya usually just walked in and started talking. This sounded serious. She picked up the folded clothes and put them on the bedside table making room for Maya, then patted the bed.

To her surprise, Maya closed the door behind her. *This really must be important.* Maya's eyes were watery, was she going to cry? Ashley reached out and touched Maya's arm. "What's wrong, hon? You okay? Did you and Sam get into a fight?"

"No." Maya blinked rapidly. "I'm just embarrassed. Sam and I are good actually, really good. That's what I wanted to talk to you about." She leaned forward and lowered her voice, as if the walls might have ears. "I need to know about birth control."

Ashley blinked; she had not been expecting that. Why hadn't she? Maya was a healthy 16-year-old girl with a steady 17-year-old boyfriend. She was in college now and her 17th birthday was fast-approaching. Of course she would be thinking about sex. Then she realized it might be more than *thinking* about sex. "Have you and Sam been sexually active?" She tried to keep her voice even, with no hint of judgment. Ashley herself had been slow to blossom sexually. Her first fumbled attempts at sex were in her twenties, but many of her friends had begun experimenting much earlier.

"No," Maya rushed to assure her. "But I promised Dad that Sam would not come between me and my education and I want to be prepared when, if..."

Relief flowed through Ashley. She exhaled in relief. "That's really smart, Maya. Uh, have you thought of talking to your dad about it?"

Maya's mouth turned down and her nose wrinkled. "No. I could have talked to Mom, I mean..." Her eyes overflowed with tears then and she brushed them away as they fell. "I could talk to her about anything involving my body 'cause she was a doctor and all. But Dad's clueless. He still thinks I'm ten years old."

Ashley nodded; she had noticed Jonathan's unrealistic view of his daughter who was very mature for her age. She felt torn. She was living in Jonathan's house, and was sort of his employee. Would he feel betrayed if she gave advice to his daughter on such a sensitive topic?

On the other hand, she felt strongly that women had a right to control their own bodies. The girl was trying to be responsible. She took a deep breath. "I'm going down to get LaRue's prescription tomorrow. I don't know if she'll take it, but I'm going to fill it. Anyway, I can call the women's clinic and get you an appointment. That way you can talk to the doctor about what form of birth control is best for you, and get all your questions answered." *And I won't be the one giving her advice.*

"That would be great, Ash. Thank you so much." Maya flew into Ashley's arms for a hug. She had done the right thing, hadn't she?

"But still, when you decide, you might want to talk to your dad. He's a pretty reasonable guy," Ashley suggested, forcing a smile, unsure if it was true.

Maya jumped from the bed. "Are we talking about the same guy?" She grinned and skipped from the room.

Ashley sat on the bed staring at her bedspread. What a week. First, dealing with LaRue's constant grousing. *The doctor told her the same thing I did, but LaRue still took it personally, like depression is some kind of personality flaw. Then, graduation, and now, Maya wants to have sex. Jeez, living here is like riding a rollercoaster of emotions, so much more complex than living alone. What would Sophia think of this crowd in her home? Two dogs, a cat, and two extra adults. I wish I'd known Sophia.* More than once she'd thought she could have used Sophia's advice. Of course, if Sophia was alive, Ashley wouldn't be in this situation.

Her phone beeped. She grabbed it from her back pocket. A text from Parker popped up. Excitement and irritation fought within her. She had not heard from him since he broke up with her. The text read "Is everyone better? Do you want to go for a run sometime?"

She stared at her phone. Just like that? No explanation, no apology. And yet, hope surged within her. She was tired of being nursemaid to a cantankerous old lady and an emotional teenager. Jonathan barely talked to her; he just worked, ate, and slept. It would be nice to have a conversation with someone her age. It didn't have to mean anything else. He was only asking her to run, not to date. They could be friends, couldn't they? She picked up her phone and hit reply. "Sure, what time?"

Chapter Forty-Four

Maya

June 18, 2020

Well, I now know more about birth control than I ever thought I would. The women's center was cool though. They treated me like an adult. The doctor gave me a ton of information and links to videos and things. Ultimately, I decided on a copper intrauterine device . . . an IUD. It's something you can leave in for years and it's not full of hormones to make me crazy. Since neither Sam nor I has ever had sex, we won't even have to use condoms or worry about STDs.

It feels weird to write this, like I want to lock my journal or hide it somewhere safe. But that's not how I felt after the doctor's visit. I actually felt like I was taking control of my life and protecting my future. The doctor seemed impressed with me. She talked about sex like it was the most natural thing in the world. Not so my Dad. Here's what happened next.

It's a clear and warm June evening. This summer has been really hot, and the evenings are the only time it feels good to sit outside. Dad is on the swing, sipping his after-dinner drink and I decide to join him. Ashley's dogs are lying on the patio's cool pavers.

"Hey," he says.

"Hey." I settle next to him, and he drapes an arm around me.

"Your birthday is coming up."

"And Father's Day." Dad and I always share our special week. He said I was the best Father's Day gift he ever got even though I came a week after Father's Day.

"You're going to be 17." He says it with this look on his face that makes me feel sad inside. Like he's thinking of Mom. I'm sad too. Mom won't be here to celebrate me. She was so great at celebrations, always buying thoughtful gifts that she squirreled away months in advance, decorating the house with a Happy Birthday banner, and making a huge Italian dinner with all of my favorite food. "Yep," I say because I can't think of anything else to say.

"What do you want for your birthday?"

"We could get my license? They are opening up for tests again."

"Right," he says. "We should do that for sure. And you can drive Mom's car. I'm sure she'd want that." He sighs.

"I miss her too, Dad."

He nods. "I want to make it a special day, but I can't cook like Mom did and the restaurants aren't open. What do you want to do for your birthday?"

"Well, Sam wants to take me on our first official date now that he has a car and a license. We'll probably make a day of it and go up to the lake. People are allowed in up there if they stay distanced. Then we'll take a picnic or find some food, I don't know."

"*Humph,*" he snorts, crossing his arms. I know I've hurt his feelings.

"Of course, we can still do something as a family." When he doesn't say anything, I should stop talking. I know Dad's moods, and when he is sad about Mom it's not the best time to try a deep conversation. But for some reason, I don't stop. "Don't you like Sam?"

"Sure, sure." He picks up the tumbler off the seat of the swing and sips his drink. "I just don't like how much time you're spending with him, that's all. You promised that your school would come first."

"I'm doing fine in my summer class, Dad. I promised I would put school first. Don't you trust me?"

"I do trust you. I just don't trust him. I know what boys his age are like. I was one."

Anger starts to flare up my spine. I know the truth of my birth though we've never discussed it—Mom was pregnant. That's why they got married. "Sam isn't like you. We will be taking precautions."

His face turns red then. I should back off, but he is pissing me off. "What do you mean, 'precautions'?"

"You don't need to worry about it, Dad. If Mom was here, we wouldn't be having this conversation at all."

A vein is pulsing in Dad's forehead. "Well she's not, so we are."

And then, I say the craziest thing. It's like the doctor has given me empowerment, but no common sense. I fly off the swing and turn on him. "What are you worried about, Dad, that I'm going to get pregnant like Mom? Well, you can rest your mind on that. I'm on birth control now and I'm old enough to have sex if I want to. You said you trusted me. Then prove it and stop asking me about it."

Shock fills his face, and he turns a deeper shade of red with rage or embarrassment, I'm not sure which. "What?" he roars. "When did you do that? Who took you? No one asked my permission. Was this Ashley's doing?" He stands slowly looking around as if looking for someone to blame.

"No, Dad, it was my doing. I'm old enough to make decisions about my own body and I don't need you to give me permission." Okay, that last part was definitely over the top, but it's out there and I can't take it back. His face crumbles as if I've said the worst thing in the world. I don't know what to do or how to fix this, so I stomp off. I try to slam the sliding glass door on my way into the house, which doesn't really work. As I pass Ashley in the kitchen, she looks at me, concern wrinkling her forehead.

"Well, I told him," I said, "and he was *not reasonable.* In fact, I'd hide if I were you." I stomp all the way up to my bedroom and slam the door for good measure, then throw myself on the bed and sob my heart out. I have made a mature decision, the doctor said so. So why do I feel like a five-year-old?

CHAPTER FORTY-FIVE

LaRue

June 2020

LaRue was getting dressed, thinking about how her new prescription was affecting her life. *Well, if that Doctor wasn't right after all. And Ashley too.* "Walter, I wish you hadn't been so damn stubborn. One week on these pills and I feel like a new woman. It's like..." She buttoned her capris, which were slightly too big after her time in the hospital, and tried to think of a description of how the anti-depressants were affecting her. "It's like the world had gone to black and white, and now the color is coming back."

There was a tap at the door and Ashley stuck her face in. "You ready?"

"Yes, just let me get my purse." LaRue grabbed her purse and put in it all the things she might need: her phone, Kleenex, and her money. She was only going over to Betty's house for coffee, but you never know. Then she grabbed her cane, quite impressed with herself for having graduated to a cane. It was so much more dignified than a wheelchair or a walker.

On the drive over, LaRue felt downright chatty. She could tell by the lift of Ashley's brows that she longed to say "I told you so," but she didn't. LaRue was glad about that.

"What do you and Maya have planned for the day?" LaRue asked.

"She wants to make all of her dad's favorites starting with roast beef and ending with chocolate layer cake, for Father's Day, so we will be in the kitchen, and he has been banished from the house.

"I thought those two were fighting."

"They seem to have made a truce. I'm not sure how it happened. It's a bit strange to be inside someone else's family, isn't it? In my family, when there was a fight everyone just acted like it never happened, but I don't think that's what's happening here."

"You got that right. Italians are much louder. I heard all that door slamming," LaRue laughed. "But it's a nice little family; I bet they'll work it out. I'll give them that much."

"True." Ashley nodded, pulling up to Betty's house. "Let me help you get up to that porch."

"I can do it. They have a handrail. I'll call you when we're done." LaRue opened the door before Ashley could protest, then took extra care up the steps so as not to prove herself wrong. Ashley waited in the car until she was all the way up. LaRue turned and gave a little wave. She could see that Betty had set up some chairs on the porch at a safe distance and laid out a plate of cookies and cups for coffee. She quickly put on her mask and knocked on the door.

Betty came to the door wearing a huge grin. "Well, look what the cat dragged in. Air-hug." The two women laughed and pretended to hug each other, squeezing themselves instead. "Have a seat. Jackie will be here any minute and I'll bring out the coffee."

Right then Jackie pulled up in her Subaru. LaRue missed driving. It wouldn't be long now. She just had to wait for the go-ahead from the doctor. Jackie was the healthiest of the three. She even played tennis and golf when her asthma wasn't acting up. "Hey, stranger," she said, bounding up the stairs and pulling out a chair. "You look great." She pulled up her mask.

"So do you," said LaRue. Jackie looked like she was sixty. It helped that she dyed her hair blonde and was so trim and athletic. The door opened and Betty came out with a tray laden with coffee, cream, and sugar on it, then joined them at the table. "I don't think we need masks since we're outside *and* six feet apart. What do you think? I never realized how much I lip read until we started wearing those darn things."

Both women agreed and pulled their masks off quickly.

"Agreed. I hate them," said Jackie. "No oxygen today?"

"Thankfully, no. I think I'm having a remission." Betty poured coffee in the mugs on the tray and handed them to her friends. "Today is a good day, and with you two here, it's even better. LaRue, you don't know how worried we were when we heard you were sick."

"You're not the only ones," said LaRue. "I was worried too."

"But you're better now?" asked Jackie.

"On the mend and covid-free. May I?" LaRue helped herself to one of Betty's famous chocolate chip cookies.

"Of course. You look like you need a little fattening up," said Betty.

"I definitely lost some weight," agreed LaRue. "But I hope to keep it off. I want to start dating."

"What?" Betty and Jackie asked at the same time, sharing surprised looks.

"Yep, I've decided that I've waited long enough. I don't think Walter would mind. Once I can walk without a cane and I move back to my house, Maya is going to do a photoshoot and help me set up an online dating profile."

"Well, I never thought I'd see the day," said Betty.

"I want to do that," said Jackie.

LaRue laughed. "I'm pretty sure Cathy would object."

"I suppose," laughed Jackie. "But it sounds fun."

"Agreed," said LaRue. It did sound fun now that she'd said it to her friends. She'd have to talk to Maya about it when she got home.

Jackie pulled a pen from her purse and a napkin from the tray. "Okay, let's brainstorm what kind of guy you're interested in and what you want to say on your dating profile. If I can't date, I want to live vicariously." They all laughed.

"Well." LaRue tapped her chin, thinking. "I don't want a grumpy old codger."

Jackie laughed. "We can't put that on your profile...what would be the opposite?"

Betty chimed in. "Someone fun, who enjoys going out."

"On adventures," LaRue clarified. "I don't need to go to bars or anything."

Jackie kept scribbling. "Okay, how's this: Looking for a young-at-heart companion for adventure."

"Oh, I like that," said LaRue. "And he's got to be a Democrat."

"Really?" said Betty. "That might narrow the field."

"I don't care," said LaRue. "Can you see me on the arm of someone in a *Make America Great Again* hat? Walter would turn over."

"Okay," said Betty. "How about progressive views preferred?"

"I guess that would do it. Oh, and he has to like cats." LaRue grabbed a second cookie.

"A must," agreed Betty.

LaRue's stomach filled with happiness as if she'd taken a sip of bubbly. Surviving covid had given her a second chance at life. She took a bite of the cookie, and wouldn't you know it, she could taste it.

CHAPTER FORTY-SIX

LaRue

June 2020

LaRue loved being back in her own home, surrounded by her furniture and knickknacks. Her pantry was greatly depleted, but she didn't mind at all. She sat in her cozy Lazy Boy chair, Hershey on her lap, and looked around. It was comforting to be here, with her own things.

Occasionally, she missed the noise and excitement of having people around, but mostly she was content. Maya came over most nights to help her cross the street for dinner with the family. LaRue always brought something to share and enjoyed having a family to prepare food for. Still, she and Hershey enjoyed their little nest, and she was getting good at walking around inside without a cane.

She heard voices coming up the walk and felt a bit giddy as the girls drew close to her front door. Today was the day. She pushed Hershey off her lap, and he stalked away, affronted. Ashley and Maya were coming over to do a photoshoot and set up her online dating profile. Her stomach flipped as if she were on a roller coaster. There was a knock at the door, and it opened before she could get there.

A grinning Maya peeked in. "Grandma, are you ready?" Warm air came in through the door with Maya. Ashley followed close behind. LaRue stood, hands on hips, as the girls entered, carrying bags of who-knew-what and giggling as if they were about to toilet paper someone's house.

"I was, but you two look like mischief on a cracker, so now I'm not so sure."

"Oh, Grandma, we're just excited," said Maya. "This'll be fun. We brought props, and make-up, and Ashley brought hair styling stuff."

Ashley held up a paper bag as if for inspection. "Where do you want to start?"

"That depends on what you want to do with me. I thought I was ready."

The girls looked LaRue up and down with pressed lips as if considering. She was wearing cream-colored slacks and a blue floral blouse. Her hair, which had not been cut since the pandemic started, was a gray bushel of curls.

Maya set her bag down, sounding like a politician. "It's just that we'd like to create several different looks, you know, some outside, some inside, different out-fits. That way, your profile will show the real you."

"The real me doesn't have fancy make-up and hair. Better to put me in a mask with a protest sign."

The girls laughed. "That's actually a good idea," said Ashley. "That will keep unwanted guys away. Let's start with that and see what else you want to try."

Those words allowed LaRue to relax. She led the girls back to her bedroom where she laid out five dif-ferent masks on her bed. "Which one?"

Maya looked at the masks LaRue had made. Five of the hundreds she'd sewn before she got covid. "This one goes well with your blouse and your political statement." She held up a blue one.

LaRue took the mask and then grabbed a "Black Lives Matter" sign off the floor from the corner of the room, where several signs were stacked. "I was in the hospital during these protests, but I'm ready for the next one. Where do you want me?"

Maya considered. "How about we go in the back-yard? It'll look like you're out protesting."

They moved from the house out the sliding glass door off the kitchen. LaRue had a small backyard, but it did boast some lovely rose bushes which filled the air with their sweet fragrance. She felt sad to have neglected them this year, but they seemed to be flour-ishing anyway. "How about in front of these?" She put on her mask and stood in front of her bright red Mr. Lincoln rosebush. These vintage roses grew as large as dessert plates, and this year they were stunning, as if they knew she needed some cheer.

"Perfect," said Maya, moving in to take pictures from different angles with her smartphone.

LaRue started to get into the spirit of the thing. She tried different poses, holding the sign in front of her, holding it up in the air, and raising her other arm to make a muscle. Ashley and Maya laughed and seemed to enjoy the fun with her.

"Okay," said Maya. "Time for a new outfit."

LaRue was ready. "What should I wear?"

"I was thinking, maybe a dress?" said Maya. "You know, something more formal so they'll know they can invite you to a Reno Philharmonic concert."

LaRue's lips pushed to the side as she considered, then she headed back into the house.

Ashley stopped her when they got back to her bedroom. "LaRue, I was wondering if I might trim your hair up a bit."

"You know how to do that?" questioned LaRue. "If I'd known that, I would have asked for a haircut a month ago. This old mop is out of control."

"Well, I'm no professional, but I'm not bad. Where should we do it?"

"The kitchen. That way, I can sweep it off the linoleum." LaRue led them down the hall again.

They set up a chair in the center of the kitchen. Maya leaned against the counter, watching as Ashley pulled a haircutting drape from her bag and fastened it around LaRue. "How did you learn to cut hair?" asked Maya.

"My mom's a beautician. She owns a beauty shop in San Francisco. I grew up in beauty shops, and she was always trying the latest hairstyles on me. Some were disasters. Some were good, though."

Ashley pulled LaRue's hair through her fingers. "How do you normally like it?"

"I guess, just like it is only shorter, less bushy, especially around my ears."

Ashley started right in like she knew what she was doing. Hair began to fall around LaRue's shoulders and onto the floor.

"Do you cut your own hair, Ashley?" asked Maya.

"I have, but it's not great. I can't wait for the shops to reopen. It's hard to trust anyone since my mom has always cut my hair, but I'm getting desperate. Or maybe I'll take a trip home. I miss my folks, and Mom could cut my hair."

"Do you cut guys' hair? My dad could sure use a cut."

"Sure, if he wants me to. I can trim yours too, Maya, if you need it. When I was in college, I cut hair for spending money. Or sometimes I'd trade for things, like one guy did my taxes and I cut his hair."

She stepped to the front of LaRue and pulled down the sides of the hair, checking the length, then made some adjustments.

"Almost done, just going to check and see if I missed anything." LaRue felt her pulling the comb through her hair as she checked and made some little snips here and there.

"Boy, you're fast," said Maya.

"It's a simple cut. I can't do the kids that want zigzags buzzed into their hair, but I can do basic cuts." She took the drape off, LaRue shaking the hair onto the floor. "Now, go give it a look and let me know if you want to change the length or anything."

LaRue went to the bathroom and examined herself. She looked so much better. Was she right to be doing this? Her stomach gave a little flip. Did she really want to meet men—strangers? There could be ax murderers out there, or men who thought she was too old or, heaven forbid, who wanted sex. Should she dye her hair like Jackie did? She straightened her back. *This is nothing, just* coffee, *that's all.* She yelled to the girls,

"Wow, I look like a new woman. I love it," coming back to the kitchen. "Thanks for sweeping up. I'll go find a dress."

LaRue had such fun being gussied up by the girls. She even let Ashley apply a little makeup. By the time they left, she was exhausted. She flopped back into her chair. Hershey glared as if he didn't recognize her. "Well, Walter, I'm committed now. I hope you don't mind. No one can replace you. That's not what I'm looking for. Just someone to talk to, and maybe watch a movie with, that's all." She wiped tears that suddenly leaked from her eyes. "That's all."

CHAPTER FORTY-SEVEN

Ashley

June 2020

"How's the family?" Parker asked as they headed off on their run on the desert path. The three dogs raced ahead of them, happy to be together again. The morning was crisp and dry. This was the third time they'd met to run in the early morning since they'd started seeing each other again. They ran early to beat the heat of the day. Ashley liked that he asked about the family. He seemed to be getting used to the idea that she lived and worked at Jonathan's.

"Things are good. Maya wanted to make a special Father's Day meal for Jonathan this month, so I helped her, and we had quite a feast: roast beef, baked potatoes, green beans, and cake. It was yummy."

"That's nice."

His answer was fine, but Ashley wondered if there might be a hint of jealousy in his demeanor. She and Parker were taking it slow. His time with Cassandra had not gone well, and when he approached Ashley about running together, she wanted to keep it at *the just friends level*, at least for a while. But was he really jealous of Jonathan? He didn't have any right to be. Did he? She pushed that thought away before it could land anywhere.

She changed the subject away from Jonathan. "LaRue is healing well and moved back into her own house. The anti-depressants seem to be working. In fact, she wants to start online dating, and we had a hysterical photo shoot with her."

"That sounds fun," he said as they headed up a hill, and she had to push herself to keep up with him. She was definitely out of shape. "I wish you still had your place."

"I miss it," she admitted. "But I love being there for Maya. She and her boyfriend are getting serious. I had to help her figure out birth control."

She hoped they might be able to talk about this and how hard it had been for Jonathan to hear, but instead, he said, "At least *someone's* getting some."

She glanced at him, but he continued to look forward. The statement rubbed her the wrong way. It seemed so juvenile. Also, was he leveling an accusation at her? "Was that supposed to be funny?"

He grinned at her. "Yes. And perhaps suggestive." He raised his eyebrows twice.

"Hmmm," she said and increased her speed. Why did this man bug her? She'd been so enamored with him before, and now it seemed they were on two different planes.

He caught up with her. "Are you mad? What did I say?"

"No," she huffed, trying to catch her breath. The trail leveled out so she could speak more easily. "I'm sorry, I'm just tired from work and school." *Why am I always apologizing? I have a right to my feelings. Don't women apologize too often?*

"That surprises me," he said a bit testily. "It doesn't seem like you do much."

She stopped in her tracks. What the actual fuck was wrong with this guy? It took him a moment to realize she had stopped, and he came back, jogging in place.

"What?" he said, frowning.

"Parker, I am working my butt off to get through school as fast as I can while taking care of LaRue, and Maya, and helping with the house."

"Okay, okay," he stopped, hands up in surrender, breathing heavily. "I'm sorry. It just seems like you're an unpaid housewife, and I can't help wondering what else you are doing for that guy?"

Heat rose in Ashley's face. "Is that what you think of me?" She blinked back the tears that threatened to fall. Nope, she was not going to be with another guy who treated her as 'less than'. She'd had enough of that with Mark. Crossing her arms, she looked him in the eye. "Parker, I thought maybe we could restart this relationship, but clearly we have different priorities right now. I'm busy, and I don't have time for your middle school attitudes or accusations." She turned and ran back down the trail. It took a minute for her dogs to realize what she was doing and follow her.

"Ashley, wait. Don't be stupid."

Stupid? That did it. She turned back to him, "And don't call me." She was done. Done with being treated like a second-class citizen by a man. She reached her car in record time and loaded the dogs, slamming the back a bit too hard. What was wrong with her that she kept attracting guys who didn't value her or her work or her intelligence? *"Don't be stupid,"* he'd said. *Ugh.* Maybe she *had* been stupid. Stupid to fall for *his* pretty face.

She drove home without even seeing the road, and when she got to the house, a dark mood followed her. She put the dogs in the backyard through a side gate and then opened the front door. Voices came from the back of the house, so she quietly closed the door and headed up the stairs, not wanting to see anyone. The voices moved into the living room. It was Jonathan and Maya. They seemed to be having a deep conversation, and she paused at the top of the stairs to eavesdrop.

"I want you to know," said Jonathan, "that I was wrong to treat you like a child. You are not a child, and I respect your decisions. I'm proud of you for taking precautions before you have – uh, sex. It's hard for me to talk about, but I was wrong, and I'm sorry."

Ashley could picture that he had pulled Maya into a hug because her words came out muffled. "Thanks, Daddy, I love you."

"I love you too, pumpkin. And no matter how grown you are, you'll always be my baby."

Ashley felt tears on her cheeks now. That's what she needed. Someone she could disagree with and makeup. Someone man enough to admit when he was wrong. Someone like Jonathan.

Maya

June 26, 2020

Sam is taking me to Lake Tahoe for my birthday. I am nervous as a cat because today might be the day we finally get to have sex. I feel fun and flirty in my matching shorts and tank top.

When Sam pulls up in his car, I am surrounded by the whole family. Ashley has her arm around me, LaRue grins from the couch, and Dad paces nervously. Even Hershey came out to rub around my ankles. You'd think I was going off to war. But they'd all been up early to celebrate me with a birthday breakfast of waffles, eggs, and bacon. I opened presents as they made toasts to me with orange juice.

Part of the problem is covid, as always. During this pandemic, nobody really goes anywhere. We stay home as much as possible. This will be the first time in four months I get to go on an outing. That, and the possibility of sex hang in the air and I am greatly relieved when Sam finally arrives. I wave and dash out the door in the warm air to meet him. As usual, he has a big grin on his face that instantly relaxes me.

He rolls down his window. "Ready, birthday girl?"

"Let's go." I toss my bag with my beach towel, sunscreen, and a book into the back seat and get in. "Nice ride."

"Thanks." He smiles. "It feels weird to be going out, doesn't it?"

"I was just thinking that. Like we're breaking the rules or something."

"Don't worry. I know of a nice secluded beach. If there are other people, it will be easy to socially-distance from them, and I brought a picnic so that we don't have to eat other people's food."

"Thanks." Have I mentioned what a thoughtful boyfriend he is?

"I hope you like squid sandwiches," he says as his eyes twinkle.

"My favorite." I laugh.

The car is not new, just new to Sam. Before that, it belonged to his brother. The old Dodge has some wear in the seats and smells like French fries and car oil. Sam begins to tell me all his dreams to fix it up as we drive. "First, I'm going to get some of those sheepskin seat covers. You know, the soft ones. Then I want to get some fun rims that spin when you drive. Maybe, someday, I'll even get it painted. What color do you think would be best? I'm thinking silver blue."

"That would look good," I say. Sam's eyes grow huge when he tells me all he wants to do to his car. All I want to do is get my license so I can drive, but his enthusiasm is contagious. "How will you pay for all that?"

"Didn't I tell you? I started a business."

"What business?"

"I'm building cheap websites for my mom's friends from her writers' group. It's easy on WordPress, and they pay me like $200 a shot."

We chat happily all the way to the lake, which is only a 45-minute drive. There Sam parks on the side of the road. "Ready for a bit of a hike?"

"Sure." He leads me off the road, down a path I didn't even know existed. It winds us down to a secluded cove, and he's right. There is only one other family there, a mom and two small kids, on the far end of the cove, so we head for the opposite side.

The air is warm, already 75°, and heading to 80°. He spreads out our blanket. Lake Tahoe is known for its beauty. It sits like a blue gem on top of a mountain. Half of the lake is in Nevada, and half's in California. We are on the Nevada side, where it's less crowded.

I take off my shorts and tank top and stretch out on the blanket like a cat in the sun in my bright yellow two-piece. I fill out the top better than I did last year. Sam gives a low whistle. "Wow, you look great. How do you already have a tan?"

I blush. "I've been working on it in the backyard. Thankfully, my Italian blood helps me tan up fast."

"I guess," he says appreciatively. "No matter what I do I'm just a Reno white boy. My skin won't tan. Burn and peel, that's me."

This gives me an excuse to take a good look at Sam as he pulls off his shirt and shorts. He is built slim, but he has broad shoulders from his years on the swim team. He looks good, even if he was about as white as a boy could be. He lays down as close to me as he can get, and my heart starts to pound. We have never been this close, wearing so few clothes.

"Do you want your present now or later?" he asks, propped on his elbow, facing me.

"Now, of course!"

He sits up quickly and rummages around in his bag. I sit up too, interested to see what he got for me. This is our first year celebrating my birthday as a couple.

"This is only half of your present. I'll give you the other half this afternoon."

That makes my stomach clench with excitement. Two presents...is one sex? Nah, that would be a weird gift. I giggle to myself, but one I'd enjoy. At least, I think I would. Yikes, the reality that this might happen is ping-ponging around in my stomach.

He pulls out a small box wrapped in a red bow. Jewelry then. I hope it isn't a ring. I'm not ready for a ring, not even a promise ring. I shouldn't have worried. I open the box and pull out a silver bracelet with charms hanging off of it. "Oh, I love it!" My brown skin looks good in silver. I prefer it over gold. I pick up one of the delicate charms.

"This one..." he lifts the first charm, "...represents your first achievement, graduation from high school." It's a tiny mortarboard. "And this one..." he holds up a little computer, "...represents your online college classes."

I laugh at that. "Where did you find these?"

"Online, of course."

"And what is this one?" The third is a spiky-looking ball. I have no clue.

He lifted it and looked seriously at me, "It's covid."

I crack up. "Covid?" I choke out.

"Hey, you survived a global pandemic."

"It's not over yet."

"True," he says, latching the bracelet onto my wrist. "But two members of your family had it, and you didn't get it, so I don't think you will. It's an important memory. And now I can get you a charm for every milestone until it's all filled up, then you can remember all of your accomplishments."

Ah, it is such a Sam-present. It is thoughtful and kind and even hints at many years to come. I kiss him. Well, one kiss leads to another, and soon we lay down and he pulls the blanket over us, and we're really getting into it when I hear a child's voice yell, "Hey mommy, what are those guys doing?"

I freeze. Sam sits up. What were we thinking? This is a public beach. There are people here—children. And the sand is getting into embarrassing places. Is this how I want my first sexual experience to be?

I sit up shyly. "Swim?" he asks. And he dashes into the water, his hands covering a visible lump in his swim shorts. I giggle at the sight, then follow more slowly. Lake Tahoe water is snowmelt and very cold. But some splashing from Sam eventually gets me all the way in. It is fun to play in the water. After a few hours of reapplying sunscreen and sand and gritty sandwiches, I feel ready to get out of the heat.

"Ready for your second present?" he asks. "I'm afraid no amount of sunscreen is working. I can feel the burn."

"Ready." It is almost 2:00 o'clock, and I wonder what else he has planned. We pick up our things, shake off as much sand as we can, and walk up to the car. "Where are we going?" My excitement mounts.

"It's a surprise." He grins, starting the car.

The road follows the edge of the lake. About a mile later, he turns to head up the mountain and keeps looking at his phone where he must have a map. Finally, we pull into the driveway next to a small cabin.

"What's this? Do you have friends who live up here?" I'm trying not to be disappointed. If we are here to visit someone it will be okay, but it's not exactly what I was hoping for.

"This," he says, gesturing to the cabin, "is the second part of your present. We have this cabin to ourselves until tomorrow at eleven." He says it while looking at his lap like he's unsure how I'll take the information.

"The whole cabin is ours?" My heart's pounding. We'd been experimenting sexually but have never gone all the way. Now I feel nervous. What if I don't know what to do? Not that he would know either, but what if I'm just bad at this?

"Yep. We have it all night." He looks up at me, and hope shines in his eyes.

The pinball machine in my stomach goes into hyperdrive. I smile back but my lips won't stop quivering.

"We don't have to do anything but hang out if you don't want to," he adds quickly.

I nod, feeling a bit of relief.

We get out of the car, and I stand staring at the small but cozy-looking cabin tucked quaintly in the evergreens. It's brown with white shutters and a pitched roof to keep the snow off. The door is tucked around back in the trees. The air smells deeply of pine. He comes around the car, takes my hand, leads me up the walkway to the front door, and then pushes in the numbers on a keypad.

"But where did you get it?" I ask as he leads me inside. The cabin has a fireplace and tall windows that look out at the pines and a little porch with chairs. There is a small kitchen and a bedroom off to each side, which makes my thighs warm. "We are staying here all night?"

"I rented it on Airbnb."

"But how did you afford it?"

"I sold my first website last week."

I'm shocked. It is a beautiful and perfect present. "Oh, Sam." I give him a big kiss then. "But I'll have to tell Dad I'm staying here. I don't know what he'll say. And I brought no clothes, and we have no food."

He laughs. His shoulders drop with relief. "I already told your dad." He pulls me to him. He told my dad? I can't even imagine that conversation. "Ashley packed you a bag of clothes, and my mom sent some groceries."

I can't believe it. No wonder my family were acting so strange when I left this morning. They all knew. My face grows hot, the whole family knew what Sam was planning. I'm not sure how to feel about that.

No sand. No people. And an actual bed. My excitement mixes with my nerves, but I'm with Sam, someone I love and trust, and I'm ready for this. It's the best present ever.

CHAPTER FORTY-NINE

Ashley

July 2020

Ashley stood in the dining room, holding a glass of iced coffee. It was hot inside, even with the swamp cooler going. She leaned over Maya's shoulder as she sat at the dining room table, looking at her laptop.

"See," said Maya. "This is why I have to monitor LaRue's dating account. This guy is obviously a prisoner. You can tell because he's so young, and look at his tattoos."

Ashley leaned in for a closer look. The man was about thirty, handsome, and smiling at the camera, shirtless. "The fact that he says he likes 'more mature women' is also a clue. *Yuck*. Delete that guy. How many of those does she get?"

"About one a week. She lets me choose who she has coffee with and set up the dates during the afternoon at the Human Bean down by the river. That way, there are people around, and it's no big commitment. Plus, they can be outside, which is safer. I mean, she's already had covid, but they are saying now there are two or three different strains. We sure don't need her to be sick again."

Jonathan came out of his bedroom, hair wet, and a towel draped across his bare shoulders. "I'm ready. Where do you want me?"

Ashley had to stifle the flirty reply that came to mind and chided herself for thinking it. She was cutting his hair, which currently stuck out around his head like an electrified hedgehog. She grinned at the sight. "Can we do it in the shade on the back porch? That way, we don't get hair all over. It won't be as hot, either." She grabbed her haircutting bag off the counter.

"You're the boss," he agreed as he picked up a chair from the dining table and headed out the back door.

"Want to watch, Maya?" Ashley asked.

"No, I've got to set up some first-meet dates for LaRue."

Ashley felt a bit nervous and had hoped Maya would be there to ease the tension. Why did this make her nervous? She'd cut Maya and Sam's hair last week, and LaRue's the week before. This was no different.

Even though Ashley took care of Jonathan when he was sick, she still felt odd touching his hair. Hair-cutting is a rather intimate thing. She went outside into the heat of the July day. The shade was nice. Jonathan sat with his back to her, looking out at the snapdragons and foxgloves in the backyard. She put the drape around him and fastened the Velcro around his neck over the towel. "How short do you want it?"

"It's so hot. I want it as short as you can get it."

"All right, short it is." She took a breath and began to comb his hair. This was no big deal. She'd cut a lot of guys' hair during college. As a nurse, she had been touching people and dealing with bodily fluids. *It's just hair. Get over yourself, Ash. What is wrong with you?*

As she combed his hair, she was impressed with the thickness. "You have good hair."

"Yeah, but it's starting to migrate back a bit."

"Not bad, though, and there isn't much gray yet."

"My dad had a lot of hair," he said.

She pulled the hair between her first two fingers and cut the guide. Men's hair was simple. Basically, it was the same length all over. You just cut a guide and then match it all over the head. She had to step close to him to see well, her stomach touching the back of his head. Warmth radiated from his body, causing her stomach to tighten and heat to reach her lower regions. Was she just lonely for a man? Horny? She wanted to touch more than his hair. He had freckles on the back of his neck. It would be so easy to bend down and kiss one. She took a breath and tried to still her heart.

Get a grip, Ash. This guy has lost the love of his life. He is ten years older than me. I need to get control of myself. Maybe it's time to set up my own dating app. Love in the time of covid is tricky. Then she remembered her train-wreck relationship with Mark, and the one with Parker that had ended badly. *I wish they had a dating app with an asshole filter.*

"So," she said to distract herself. "How's work?"

"Oh, same old thing. We have more work than we can handle. People in California realized they can work from home, and don't need to pay $3,000 a month for a one-room apartment. Now, they're all moving to Reno, and that means we have to build more houses and apartments. I don't see that changing even if the economy does crash from this virus."

Good. Keep him talking. Keep your mind from thinking about him as a man, Ash. He's Maya's dad. That's all.

"How's school," he asked her. "I've noticed how good you are at studying. It's been great for Maya to see your example. I appreciate all you're doing for our family."

Dammit, why did he have to be so nice? That was not helping at all.

CHAPTER FIFTY

Maya

July 19, 2020

July 4th was canceled. Well, the fireworks anyway. Everything is canceled. No Aces Baseball, no fireworks, no nothing. *Yuck.* At least I have Sam. What would I be doing this summer without him?

Today I got to hang out with him 'cause his folks are at work. They go in a couple of days a week now; very distanced and safe, they say. So far, no one in Sam's family has been sick.

I walk over to his house in the khaki shorts and red tank top I ordered online. I would feel cute if it wasn't so hot. My hair is pulled back off my neck in a ponytail. Heat shimmers off the sidewalk, and my backpack sticks to my back.

I knock on Sam's front door. His house is more modern than ours. That's one thing I love about our neighborhood. Each house is different. There's nothing cookie-cutter about this part of town.

Sam opens the door and air conditioning rushes out toward me. It feels amazing. His smile has its usual effect on me, causing the butterflies that took up residence in my stomach ever since I've known him to flutter to life. He opens the door wide with a sweeping gesture for me to enter. "You ready?"

"Yep, I think I've got it figured out." I pull off my backpack, tugging my damp shirt off my back, and follow him into the living room. His laptop sits on a coffee table in front of a leather couch. I take my computer from my backpack and sit it on the table next to his, swiping the mouse pad to wake it up. Today we are finalizing our college classes for the first semester.

Sam sits on the couch and I plop down next to him. My bare legs tingle at the cool of the leather and stick to it. The air is almost too cold on my arms, but it's refreshing and quickly dries my sweat. I'm used to my house, which is so old and large that the swamp cooler has a hard time keeping up with Reno's intense summer heat. I tap my keyboard to bring up the schedule I worked on last night. "My dad vetoed half the classes I wanted to take."

"Like what?"

"Oh, you know Art, Drama, Basket-weaving." I laugh. "But I do get to take yoga and Japanese, so that will be fun. There are just so many great things to learn. I got a bit carried away the first time I made up the schedule."

Sam grins at me. "I'm taking jewelry-making. I had to put something fun in mine too. But the rest are pretty basic."

"Let me see." I lean into him to see his screen, and his arm goes around my back. It feels good there. I look up and catch his face close to mine. He leans in for a kiss. He tastes like wintergreen, his favorite gum. He leans me back against the back of the couch and presses the kiss further, his hand reaching up under my tank top and sending shivers down my legs. I put my hand on top of his to still its path and pull back.

"Sam, we decided we needed to do less kissing and more college prep, remember?"

He keeps his hand where it is as he breathes, "But kissing is so much more fun."

"Agreed." I sit up, pushing him off. He is right about that, so right, but I really need to clear my head, fast. "There's something I need to tell you."

He jerks back, fear in his eyes. Does he think I'm breaking up with him or something? I smile to reassure him. "It's not bad. It's just that as things are relatively safe now, my dad is taking me to Italy before school starts, to say goodbye to Mom and my grandparents."

"When? For how long?" He seems so sad about the idea of me leaving.

"If I could, I would pack you in my suitcase. We're going next week. Ashley says the word in the medical community is that fall will bring a resurgence of the virus, so we need to go now. We'll only be gone a week."

"Oh," Sam's face relaxes as he brushes back the hair that has escaped from my pony. "How do you feel about going to see – you know, their graves?"

I flop back against the couch. How *do* I feel? "Mostly I try not to think about it. It's weird to think Mom is buried in a whole other country. I'll never have a grave to visit here." Saying that out loud leaves me feeling empty. I blink back tears. "It will be hard. But good, I guess. She is buried next to my grandparents. My uncle will meet us, and we'll stay with him and his family, then he'll take us to the cemetery. I can't believe it's been six months. So much has happened since then."

"This year has felt like a decade already," he agrees.

"She never even got to meet you." Now I can't stop the tears. "She would have loved you."

"Uh-oh." He wipes tears off my cheeks. "You're making me want to kiss you again." So, he does, and I kiss him back.

CHAPTER FIFTY-ONE

LaRue

July 2020

LaRue's first coffee date was a bust. She went early to the coffee shop by the Truckee River, got an iced tea in a plastic glass, and set herself on the side of the building in the shade. She texted Robert, who "...enjoyed the outdoors and cool nights by the fire," and told him to look for her in her blue-flowered blouse.

He rode up on a ten-speed, wearing biking shorts that outlined his thin frame, a T-shirt, and a helmet with sunglasses obscuring his face. He removed his glasses but did not dismount, keeping his six feet distance. The two just stared at each other. "LaRue?" he asked; the look on his face could only mean disappointment.

Was he really 75? He looked no older than a fit fifty. "Yes," she said, with a slight frown. What would they possibly have in common?

"You mentioned you liked the outdoors..." he ventured nervously.

"I meant that I like to putter in my garden."

He smiled then, and they both nodded in understanding. "Well, good luck then," and he rode off, just like that.

She was only slightly hurt. "I mean, really, Walter, what a mismatch." She picked up her tea and headed to her car, muttering to herself. "Likes the outdoors? I'll have to have Maya fix that right away." She drove straight home to call Jackie, and they laughed together about her first "date."

"Shortest date in history," said Jackie.

"Thankfully," agreed LaRue. She chuckled about it all afternoon, and when she told the family over dinner, they joined in her glee. This online dating was going to be the most interesting thing about 2020.

Her second date was disappointing for a different rea-son. Hank met her at the same table with his cof-fee. He looked like he'd done some hard living. The smell of cigar smoke wafted over her as he sat at her table, even though she'd specified a non-smoker. *Don't judge,* she warned herself. He was not half-bad looking. He was wearing long shorts, black socks, and sandals. His Hawaiian shirt pulled tightly about his round belly.

"Well hello, gorgeous," he greeted. "You must be LaRue."

"And you must be Hank."

"You bet your sweet boopie."

She chuckled. He seemed to have a lot of energy, which was good, but she didn't think he'd be climb-ing Mt. Rose anytime soon, with the smoking and the paunch. He was a talker, jumping in to tell her about his time in the service—Korean War—and how he didn't see any of his kids anymore after a nasty divorce. He didn't ask much about her and seemed to dodge questions about what exactly he'd retired from. When she asked what part of town he lived in, he gestured vaguely toward downtown. LaRue knew there weren't many homes down there, mostly weekly hotels.

When he did ask personal questions, it was about her finances.

"So, my beauty, did you retire well?'

"What do you mean?"

"Do you have your own place? A cushy retirement package and all?"

LaRue felt a check in her gut. He was interested in her pension? She dodged that question by asking him to tell her more about his time in the war, which he seemed happy to do.

After an hour of his ramblings, LaRue stood up, taking her empty drink cup, and bowed her head toward him in a covid goodbye. "It was nice meeting you, Hank." She turned to leave.

"Well, wait." He stood quickly. "We should go to dinner. Some of the casinos are open. I could meet you at The Club."

He was referring to a small, seedy casino popular with locals who came for the free pie. She and her girlfriends had tried it once and still talked, aghast, about how anyone could ruin pie. "Hank, I think this is a no for me. But it was nice to meet you."

She headed as fast as she could for her car and locked the doors. When she got home, she ask Maya how to block a phone number. She'd bet Hank didn't have two dimes to rub together. Not that money was the only consideration, but something about him felt shady, and if she'd learned anything in her 75 years it was to trust her gut. *I guess you gotta kiss a lot of frogs...*

Her third date was more hopeful. A slender man named Clarence came to her table. "Oh," he said with a pout. "I was supposed to buy you coffee. It looks like you beat me to it." He had a friendly smile and, if you ignored his combover, he wasn't bad to look at.

They talked congenially for the whole hour. Clarence was divorced twice. He'd also had covid, but a less severe case than LaRue's, and he was healthy now. He told her of his love of fishing, his boat, and his cabin at the lake. They had such a pleasant visit she agreed to a second date on which he bought her takeout burritos, and they ate them on a blanket by the river. He was easy to be with and enjoyable. They even talked on the phone a couple of times.

Then he asked if she wanted to go up to the lake to see his cabin, and she agreed. She didn't feel he was threatening in any way, but Jonathan insisted that she drive her own car to meet him there and keep her phone on.

Her GPS took her to the lake, which, as it turned out, was not Lake Tahoe, but Washoe Lake, a lake about fifteen miles from Reno that grew or shrank depending on the amount of snowmelt off the mountain. Well, she'd just assumed he'd meant Lake Tahoe, hadn't she?

When she turned off the road, LaRue grew a bit nervous. It didn't look like an area with cabins. Her anxiety increased when the GPS stopped her in front of a small shack. She got out of the car, thinking perhaps this was a storage shed and the cabin was closer to the water. Clarence came around the building to greet her, waving happily. She relaxed a bit.

"Here it is." He beamed. "Been in the family for a long time. It's not much, but it's a great place to get away and be quiet with the fish." He was gesturing toward the shack. LaRue tried to keep an open mind. He seemed quite proud of the place. Maybe the inside was better.

He took her hand and led her around to the front. Warped steps led up to the front door. A wooden rocking chair sat on the small porch. He opened the door, which led to a small dark room. It had a couch, a dusty-looking Lazy Boy chair, and a small fireplace. She looked around for a kitchen and saw none. There was a hot pot and a hot pad on a shelf next to the bathroom.

"Cozy, isn't it? Can I get you a cup of coffee?"

"Sure," she said for want of else to say.

The room was bare except for some pictures hanging crooked on the wall of Clarence with different fish. He noticed her looking. "Aren't those great? Most of them were from Pyramid Lake. I love to fish there."

Clarence was a nice guy. He was very positive, in fact, but fishing wasn't really her thing. Walter wasn't into fishing; she'd never been exposed. That didn't mean she couldn't learn. It might be good to try something new.

"Have a seat." He gestured to the couch.

She sat down and almost sank to the floor. *"Uff."* The air whooshed out of her.

"Oops. Should have warned you about that. It's an old couch." He smiled. "Not too bad to sleep on, though. I practically live here in the summers." He took a Styrofoam cup off the shelf. "Cream and sugar?"

"Please." She glanced around, noting the sleeping bag and pillow piled up in the corner. The place smelled musty. She looked up in time to see him pour instant coffee, powdered creamer, and sugar from tall cardboard cylinders into her cup and stir it with a plastic spoon.

"Would you like to drink it here or walk on down to the lake?"

"Oh, let's walk." She was grateful to escape the small dark space. "I may need help getting up, though."

He laughed, put the cups down, and gave her a pull off the couch. When she stood, he looked at her longingly as if he might want to kiss her. She ducked around him, taking three quick steps over to the shelf and grabbing the coffees.

His face fell. He opened the door and took his cup. She sipped her coffee as they walked. It may have been the worst cup of coffee she'd ever tasted, but she smiled and followed him down a long winding path that eventually led to a rickety dock. Tied up to the doc was a small rowboat. "There she is," he boasted.

Okay, she thought. *This is my fault. He said boat and cabin, and I heard speedboat and Tahoe. He's a nice guy, easy to be around, and lonely. But he's not for m e.*

"Can I take you for a row?" he asked hopefully.

"Oh my, no. I'm not much of a water person."

They enjoyed a few more hours walking around the lake, and she could see the appeal, even if it wasn't for her. When she felt she'd been there long enough, she told him she had to get back home.

"Thank you for sharing your little bit of heaven with me, Clarence."

His smile radiated joy. She needed to let him down easy. "The thing is, you deserve someone who enjoys fishing, and unfortunately, it's not me. I don't fish. I don't even like to eat fish. But I hope you find that person. You're a very nice man."

He nodded grimly and walked her back to her car. She hugged him goodbye and was very glad to leave. *Enough of online dating. I'd rather be alone.*

CHAPTER FIFTY-TWO

Maya

August 3rd, 2020

Dad and I stand in front of my mother's grave, in a graveyard in Naples, Italy, next to a large Catholic church. It's a muggy afternoon and the air smells of moss. Mom rests next to Nonna and Nonno. My uncle Sergio stands beside Dad, weeping as he explains in lightly accented English, "I'm so sorry. We had no choice. Usually, when someone dies, we have thirty days to bury them, but when 17,000 people died at once, they only gave us five days to claim the bodies. If we hadn't already had this plot in the family, they might have been taken to one of the communal graves. They would not let us send Sophia to you. They wouldn't even let us have a funeral—just the priest. I had to make a decision right away. It was terrible."

Dad laid a hand on my uncle's shoulder. "We understand, Sergio. There was nothing else you could do. I appreciate it." Then my uncle is sobbing in my father's arms. He'd lived through hell, I realize as I watch him cry. He and his wife watched his parents and his sister die before their eyes. They had to make all the decisions without any help from us. I wiped the tears that had been leaking from my eyes since we got on the plane to come here. Dad, however, remains stoic. Will he ever cry?

Aunt Anita slips her arm around my waist. She is a short lady, and her English is heavily accented, but she is very kind. Her children, Carmen, and Paulo, who are eight and ten, stand next to her, wide-eyed and nervous. They glance back and forth between us all. Dad once told me about what soldiers looked like coming back from the war. He called it 'shellshock'. This must be what shellshock looks like. The whole country is in shock. People walk around like zombies, grief etched on their faces like they still can't believe what happened to them.

I'm having trouble knowing how to feel. I miss my mom. Being here brings it all right back to me. But I also feel sad about my relatives. I can see what a toll this pandemic has taken on them, on the whole country. It makes me want to flee back to America, where people keep their emotions buttoned up inside and don't wear them so visibly on their faces. Which way is better? Maybe if we cried more, we'd heal faster. I don't know.

That night my uncle organized a wake. It is in the piazza, which is a communal square outside his house. Everyone arrives wearing masks; people come by with flowers and food. As the night wears on, the masks look more like neck ornaments. I'm glad we are outside because soon social distancing is a thing of the past. There is a lot of drinking. I sit with my cousins in fold-out chairs, and people come by speaking their condolences in broken English and Italian. It is a strangely solemn, yet happy, affair. As people drink more, it gets louder, and there is more laughter, and even singing. My cousins eventually run off to play with friends. I go to stand by my dad, who occasionally puts his arm around me and squeezes my shoulder. He lets me drink wine, which somehow tastes better than the wine at home, and soon I begin to feel fuzzy-headed and numb.

By the end of the evening, Dad has to hold onto my shoulder to get upstairs in my uncle's house. We are sleeping in my cousins' twin beds. And I fall quickly asleep after the exhausting day. But I wake in the middle of the night. The sound I hear is the agony of a trapped animal. It takes me some time to figure out what it is. Dad is weeping into his pillow. My heart breaks. I slip out of bed and go over to him, gently placing my hand on his back. He turns to me, sits up, and gasps, "I'm sorry."

I put my arms around him. It feels awkward at first, but then he hugs me tight, and we both cry. It is the worst and the best thing because somehow, I know we'd been treading water since Mom died, unable to move forward, stuck in a strange kind of limbo. But now, as we hold each other in that tiny room in Naples, it's as if there is solid ground under our feet.

As if we can begin to climb out of the ocean of our grief and move toward the shore.

CHAPTER FIFTY-THREE

Ashley

August 2020

Ashley sat across from her mother on the velvety softness of her parents' loveseat. It felt good to be back in the Bay Area where the moist air was gentle on her skin. As soon as Maya and Jonathan left for Italy, and LaRue assured her she was fine on her own, she hit the road for a visit home. She needed a haircut, and someone to talk to.

Her mother, still beautiful at sixty, took a sip of her coffee. Her legs were pulled up under her, the three times a-week yoga practice keeping her as limber as a much younger woman. "Tell me about school."

Ashley sighed. "I finished the first two quarters. It's ideal not to have to work right now. I can give it most of my time. Pharmacology was a bear, though. I'll get through another quarter this fall and then start my precepting in January."

"Where will you do that?"

"I'm not sure. Since the pandemic, some of the students have been unable to find placements. Doctors are too busy to take on students. It's a circular problem. They need more of us in the field but can't take the time to train us."

Her mom brushed her silver hair behind an ear. Ashley liked her mom's natural hair. She'd dyed it most of Ashley's life, saying her clients expected it, but during the pandemic, she had let it go gray, and the result was a lovely silver. It was a gutsy move for a beautician, but her mother told her that many of her clients were doing the same. When the shop opened again, she could help them blend their outgrowth in. "I worry about you working with people in hospitals to get your hours. Maybe you should just wait a bit. They are working frantically on a vaccine."

"Well, I'll be as careful as I can. I've certainly been exposed already. Thankfully I didn't get it from Jonathan or LaRue. Or maybe I'm one of those people that got it and had no symptoms."

"You've created quite a little family for yourself there in Reno. I must say I'm a bit jealous. We miss you."

"I miss you too, Mom. But I love Reno. Maybe you and Dad should sell the house and the salon. With what you could get for this house, you could buy one of those McMansions in Reno. Jonathan says house prices are rising, so you'd better hurry."

They laughed. It felt good to laugh with her mom. Why had she stayed away so long? Mark had never wanted to come with her and didn't like her going without him. Then the pandemic hit, and she'd stayed put. She looked around the room. The wood floors gleamed, the white rug under the coffee table looked new, but everything else was familiar. The place was cozy but artistically decorated. She shivered.

"Are you cold, Ash?" Mom took a throw blanket off the back of the couch and handed it to her.

"Thanks, I forget how cold San Fran feels in the summer." Ashley's mind jumped to Mark Twain's famous saying, "The coldest winter I ever spent was a summer in San Francisco." She didn't repeat it though; her mom had heard it too many times.

Her mother touched her leg. "I worry that you're becoming too attached. What happens when you graduate? Maya will be going off on her own soon. Jonathan might want his house back. Are you perhaps getting overfond of . . . the situation?"

Tears flooded Ashley's eyes. Her mother could read her, all right. Mom scooched closer and took her hand and waited while Ashley let the tears fall. Finally, she reached for a box of tissue behind her and handed it to her daughter. "Tell me."

"Oh Mom, I think I'm falling in love with him. He's good and kind, and a great dad..."

"Then what's the problem?"

"Well, his wife, whom he adored, just died, for one thing. And he's ten years older than me, for another."

"Age doesn't matter at this point, Ashley. Think about your Aunt Casey."

Ashley's aunt, her mom's younger sister, had married a guy twenty years older and it seemed to work for them, although Ashley thought there might be trouble later. Forty-five and 65 were different from 65 and 85. How would that be as she and Jonathan aged? She shook herself for thinking of herself and Jonathan as a couple.

Her mom shifted on the couch. "But does he feel the same way? Has he said anything or given you any sign?"

Ashley shook her head. "No, he doesn't know, no one knows. I feel like a heel for even thinking about him. He's in Italy right now to visit his wife's grave for the first time. I can't say anything."

Her mother rubbed her thumb over Ashley's palm, a calming gesture she'd always used when Ashley was a girl. "Then it's better just to wait. You'll have to be patient. This pandemic is changing all the rules, though. Life is short, and I think everyone realizes that..."

The front door opened and her father came in, tall and handsome, with a bounce in his step. He set down two woven bags full of food. "Where's my honey badger?"

He was wearing a mask and his eyes sparkled, his arms spread wide. Ashley jumped off the couch and ran into his arms. The hug felt good, and warm, and smelled of fresh air. It had been so long since she'd been touched – since Parker, that fateful night, and one or two quick hugs from Maya. Dad held her at arm's length, inspecting her face. "Are you okay, sweetie?"

"Yes, Dad, just homesick."

"Can I take off this mask?"

"Yes. I tested negative before I came down."

"Thank God. I get so tired of this thing." He ripped the mask off his face, hung it on a hook by the door, then removed his jacket. "Your mother says removing a mask is the modern equivalent of how a woman feels taking off her bra at the end of the day."

She laughed. It felt good to be home. She could relax. She could breathe, and hopefully, she could take a little time to sort things out.

CHAPTER FIFTY-FOUR

LaRue

September 2020

The leaves were turning. The air was crisp in the mornings and warm in the afternoon. In LaRue's opinion, September was Reno's best month. It was predictably warm and beautiful. If not for the virus, and the smoke pouring in from wildfires, things would be perfect. The virus swept through Reno once more with a vengeance. LaRue was glad that Jonathan and Maya were home safely from Italy, but sad that all university students had been sent home so Maya was again studying from the computer screen. It was not the freshman year she'd envisioned for the girl.

Ashley had returned from her time with her parents with a fresh hairstyle. She seemed more peaceful and dove headfirst into her studies, as well. Meanwhile, watching Ashley's dogs for those three days had been a bit rough. They'd dug up some of LaRue's backyard, and she'd spent the following weeks repairing the damage.

Life was settling back into a manageable cadence for LaRue, and fall meant only one thing for her: getting out the vote. She had been volunteering to make phone calls every week. They had to get folks out to vote. This was the most important election she could ever remember.

She looked at her watch. "Time to go, Hershey. You hold down the fort, okay?" The cat scowled. She pushed herself out of the chair and grabbed a jacket off the hook by the door. "Let's see." She dug through her mask basket pulling one out. "Here's a festive fall mask." The mask had bright fall leaves against a black background, and she shoved it into her pocket. Masks, she realized, were not just good for the virus, but also helped protect against the smoke in the air. She grabbed her purse and left the house.

Her car wasn't getting much use since the pandemic began, but the traffic seemed to be back to its irritating normal. Had the Californians moving in brought this new aggressive driving? She was glad she only had one exit up the freeway to get to Betty's house. Betty was hosting the meeting for their part of town. Jackie would be there today, too. She was in charge of organizing the Democrats in her area. She had so much energy. This would be fun. It was almost like before the pandemic.

LaRue parked at the curb outside Betty's house and left her jacket in the car. It was warming up nicely, but she could taste the smoke that hung in the air. She worried that it would irritate Betty's COPD and Jackie's asthma. There were only a few cars today. She didn't blame people for not wanting to go out. If she hadn't had the virus already, she might not be here either. Reno, set in a valley, was thick with smoke from California wildfires for the second summer in a row. What was burning now?

She climbed the stairs up to the porch and secured her mask. A sign on the door said, "The meeting is in the backyard" with an arrow pointing around the house. *Glad I'm not having trouble with stairs any-more,* thought LaRue climbing back down. It was smart to have the meeting outside, safer on all ac-counts.

Betty had a nice backyard. Chairs had been set up on the patio in a horseshoe pattern facing the cement porch where Jackie stood now. LaRue walked up to greet her friend.

Jackie turned toward her, clipboard in hand, wear-ing an N95 mask. They were hard to come by as the emergency workers needed them, but with Jackie's asthma, she needed one too. Should she even be out-side?

"LaRue, good to see you. Take a seat, we'll start soon."

Jackie was all business when she was in charge. Betty was wiping the seats of the folding chairs with san-itizer. She'd found an N95 mask too. "Got you on clean-up, have they?"

Betty nodded. "Here, take some. People are starting to arrive." She handed LaRue a few of the wiping cloths. "Do that row, by Ian. Did you meet Ian? He's new here. Better go greet him." She gestured to a man who was already seated and talking to another fellow whom LaRue recognized. Bob Clark.

"I haven't met him yet," said LaRue. Jackie had made greeting new people LaRue's unofficial job at these meetings. Betty's eyes crinkled in a smile and suggestively raised her eyebrows, causing LaRue to glance back to where Ian sat. He was laughing behind his mask as he talked to Bob. He looked friendly. She rolled her eyes at Betty and walked over to his chair.

"Hello." She smiled down at him. "I'm LaRue. I don't believe we've met. Hi, Bob."

"Hi, LaRue," Bob said. "This is Ian. Well, I'd better get back to my seat. Nancy looks lost." He headed back to his wife. LaRue had heard that Nancy was dealing with dementia, and she did look a bit confused, poor thing.

"Well, good morning to ya," Ian said, meeting her eyes. His were a startling Tahoe-blue. "It's nice to meet you. I'd shake your hand but it's prohibited."

She laughed. He had a lilt to his voice. Was he Irish? The chairs were set out six feet apart; she knew Jackie had measured. She wiped down her row and then sat in the one nearest him. "Is that an accent I hear?"

"Aw, you found me out." He gazed at her, and she longed to see what was behind the mask. His hair was a nice salt-and-pepper, and his collared shirt looked clean and pressed under a blue knit vest. "I'm from the Emerald Isle originally, been here most of my life, though."

"How fun." LaRue thought he had a very kind face, what she could see of it. "Are you new to Reno? Betty said you were."

"No, not new to Reno. My wife and I retired here about eight years ago, from California, like everyone else." His eyes sparkled.

Disappointment flooded her. He had a wife.

As if he'd read her mind, he continued. "Then, two years ago, she up and left me. Can you believe it?"

"Left you?"

"Cancer," he said. She could see the pain in his eyes and knew it too well. "And the kids said I needed to get my arse out of the house and do something good for somebody else. So here I am."

"I lost my husband to cancer too, ten years ago."

He gave her a nod. It was a look she knew. Those who'd lost a loved one to the ravages of cancer had lived through a terrible initiation to the club no one wanted to join. She didn't have to wonder about his political affiliation; this was a Nevada Dems meeting. That made her smile.

"It's taken me a while to feel like I could move on, ya know?" he said.

"I certainly know." She wiped the smile from her face so he wouldn't misinterpret it, then realized he couldn't see it anyway. "Sadly, I do."

"But you didn't remarry? Or am I getting too personal?"

She laughed. "No I did not. Although I tried online dating recently."

He shrunk away as if from a bad smell. "And how was it? My daughter's been pushing me to try it."

She shook her head. "I hated it. It made me feel desperate and unnatural, like wearing clothes two sizes too small."

He laughed so heartily he had tears in his eyes. It made her laugh too.

Then it was as if she heard Walter say *I like him*. Her breath caught in her throat, and her eyes glistened as she glanced down. Had her husband just given her his approval?

Jackie came up to their row. "I'm cutting this meeting short because of the smoke. I'm pairing up folks who are willing to walk a neighborhood, masked and distanced and all. Might you two team up for that?"

LaRue smiled, were her friends working together to set her up? She glanced at Betty who, of course, was watching, wiggling her eyebrows at LaRue. Before she could say anything, Ian said, "I'd be glad of a nice fall stroll with this lovely lady, if she's up for it."

Warmth filled LaRue's chest. "I'd love to."

Chapter Fifty-Five

Maya

September 22, 2020

When I get back from Italy, Sam and I turn into rabbits. I can't help it. It's the only thing that makes me feel better, to be with him that way. We've christened his parents' couch, and his bedroom, and even managed my bedroom when everyone was out. It's like I can't get enough of him. Like he's all that is grounding me to the earth.

I wonder when I go down to UNR for a lab if people can tell. Do I look like someone who's just had sex? I've got to say it feels awkward to go to school. Almost all of our classes are online, but the labs are hands-on classes, so we have to attend in person. The college is close enough to my house to walk down. Today I bundled up in my favorite fall scarf and one of Mom's sweaters. Dad doesn't seem to mind me wearing her clothes, although sometimes he looks at me a bit wistfully.

I'm wearing my skinny jeans and Ugg boots. I don't care if they look bougie, Mom bought them for me last Christmas, and damn it, they are cozy. The wind is picking up and sending an icy chill through me, so I tighten my thrift-store corduroy blazer around me. It's a ten-minute walk past students' rented houses and dorms onto the campus. The campus is old, and a mixture of beautiful brick buildings, green lawns, and modern statues. Today I'm going to the science lab. It's in the new Davidson Math and Science building. It's a huge building with about a thousand labs. The class is small, only 24 students, which feels safe. We are all separated from each other, and masked. By the time I get there my body has warmed up so I shed my blazer and climb into my chair.

This class is taught by a teaching assistant whose English is hard to understand, especially through a mask. Truthfully, I'm having trouble concentrating on my studies. Guilt sweeps through me. It's like my mom's biggest fears are coming true. All I want to do is be with Sam—all the time. I mean, the world is on fire, and everyone is dying, why should I care about school? I know that's not what Mom would want for me, but she's not here. *She's not here.* And it pisses me off.

When class is over, I stuff my notebook into my bag and decide to skip my next class. It's Humanities, online, and stupid anyway. I head up the hill to Sam's house. It's warmed up a lot and I'm carrying my blazer and have stuffed my scarf into my backpack. I bet college used to be fun. I bet people made all their friends-for-life in that first year. I've met no one. It's depressing.

I ring Sam's doorbell. He comes to the door and gives me a tired smile. I can tell by the papers he has spread out on the table behind him he's been studying. "Didn't expect to see you. Don't you have classes today?"

"Anyone home?"

"Nope, they're working today."

I walk past him, grabbing his hand as I go, pulling him down the hallway to his bedroom. He lets go, rushing back to lock the front door, then follows me down the hall. "I guess we're doing this."

Chapter Fifty-Six

LaRue

October 2020

Ian arrived at her door precisely at 2:00 o'clock to pick her up for canvassing. LaRue did love a punctual man. In her family it was, *If you're on time, you're late.*

She'd dressed with care for the cooler weather, with her brown slacks, green turtleneck, and beige cardigan. Her fall leaf mask tied the whole outfit together. Ian rang the bell and LaRue took a breath before opening it. His beautiful eyes lit up, in what must have been a smile under his mask.

"Hello, Lass. Are you ready to wow the constabulary?"

She laughed, pretty sure they'd not be wowing anyone today. "As ready as I'll ever be."

He looked quite nice. He had on a light woolen topcoat and a matching hat. He was a dapper dresser. His mask even matched his coat. As they walked to the driveway, he opened the car door for her, and she appreciated that. It was a nice car, a very clean white Lexus. When she'd fastened her seatbelt, he showed her a printout of a map of the houses they were supposed to canvas to ask people if they were registered to vote. "There are only about 25," he said, tapping the map. "If we get these done, we can catch an early dinner. By the way, do you think we can take these off when we're in the car?" He pointed to the mask.

"Sure." She removed its strings from around her ears letting it dangle, grateful for the mask chain Jackie had given her. It was a chain like people used for reading glasses. "I'm well and haven't been exposed to anyone sick. How about you?"

"Fit as a fiddle." He grinned.

They stared at each other. It was the first time they'd seen each other's faces. She realized you can't tell what a person looks like without seeing their mouth. He had a very kind face, with a salt-and-pepper beard that framed his jaw and connected to a neatly trimmed mustache. She smiled; he was quite handsome. He smiled back so she relaxed, having passed some kind of test as well.

They drove to the first neighborhood, where she assured him she could get out of the car without him running around to open the door every time. "Though it's a very nice gesture."

It was a well-kept middle-class neighborhood, and a time of day when people who were retired or had kids in school might be home. Most people were reluctant to open the door at all; thank you, pandemic. Those who did, opened it just a crack. It was obvious the canvassers weren't going to be invited in to chat with anyone today.

At the fourth house, they got their first meanie. A gruff-looking fellow opened the door and glared at them. "What do you two libtards want?"

LaRue was taken aback, unable to speak, but Ian poured on Irish charm. "Oh, kind sir, we are just out encouraging people to register to vote. Would you happen to be registered?"

"Of course, I'm registered. I stand by our president. It's obvious who you two are voting for, with those masks on. Don't you know this whole thing is a hoax by the liberal Democrats to take our minds off of the real issues?"

LaRue felt sick to her stomach. The pandemic was a worldwide health crisis. No one American political party could have started it. That didn't make any sense at all, besides, if this was a hoax, it was one that had almost killed her. "I've had covid, sir, and I can promise you it is no hoax. I almost died."

"Well," he insisted as he began to close the door, "you just had a bad case of the flu, that's all." *Slam.*

Ian and LaRue looked at each other in shock. He put his hand on her arm. "Don't let it get to you, lass. He's just one grumpy old man with his kilt in a twist. Probably scared, like the rest of us."

LaRue wanted to believe that, but as they continued their rounds they faced more slammed doors, scared faces, as well as occasional bits of guarded kindness. This pandemic was changing the world from something she loved to something she didn't recognize. She had thought that facing a global crisis together would bring the country together, like it had on September 11th, yet it seemed to be separating people more than ever. The best part of the day was just being with Ian. He had a positive outlook on life and kept up a witty banter the whole day.

After their last house, Ian helped LaRue into the car. Weariness hit her. Covid fatigue seemed to sneak up on her like that sometimes. "Whew, that was harder than I pictured."

He turned his sparkling eyes on her and smiled. "Agreed, we need to celebrate."

"Celebrate what? The downfall of America?"

"No, we need to celebrate democracy. We did something today for democracy. We left information on people's doorknobs about how to register to vote. If we sign up one voter, it will have been worth it."

"I must say, Ian, I like your attitude." This man was undauntable.

"Now, where do you want to go? Any fast food joint with a drive-thru or restaurant with outdoor seating is on the menu."

"Hmm," she searched her mind for something fun. "Have you ever been to Red Robin? They have yummy shakes and hamburgers. I could use a strawberry shake. I don't think they have outdoor seating, though."

"I tell you what I'll do, I'll call and see if they have curbside pickup. If they do, we can eat in my car. It will be like an indoor picnic."

She was shocked that he wasn't afraid to eat in the car. Walter had always been a neat-freak about his car. This guy was growing on her. She hoped she'd get to see him again.

CHAPTER FIFTY-SEVEN

Ashley

October 2020

When Ashley returned from San Francisco she felt a change in the house, at least with Johnathan. He seemed different, lighter. She thought a lot about what her mom said. Maybe she should tell Jonathan how she felt. Maybe he felt the same way. But would it ruin the friendship they were building? She had to live in the same house with him for a few months yet; what if he didn't feel the same way and things got awkward?

Thankfully, it was easy to hide in her schoolwork. Grad school was intense . . . and then there was Maya. Couldn't put her finger on it, but the girl was acting different, like a shade had closed behind her eyes. Ashley wondered if things were okay with her and Sam.

She sat on the couch hoping to catch Maya when she came downstairs for a little girl talk. When Maya came down, she had her backpack slung over her arm and headed straight for the door. "Maya," Ashley called.

Maya paused, looking irritated. "Yeah?"

"I thought maybe you'd like to take a study break with me and go to Starbucks for coffee or something?"

"Can't. I'm going to Sam's to study."

"I just wondered if you're okay, you seem a bit, um, stressed since you came back from Italy."

Maya didn't even look up at her. "I'm good," she said walking out the door.

Ashley sat on the couch feeling helpless. Maya was not her daughter, but she felt that if her mother were here, she would definitely do something. Maya had said her mom was very strict. How would she feel if she knew Maya was spending so much time with Sam? She didn't know what her place was in this family. Should she say something, or let it go? She was supposed to be keeping an eye on Maya, but that was pretty hard now that the girl was never home.

She decided to try to talk to Jonathan about it when he got home from work. She'd make him a nice meal and then maybe they could talk.

When Jonathan came home, she had steaming enchiladas waiting. After he cleaned up, he sat across from her. "This looks amazing, thank you. Any special occasion?"

"No, I just thought it might be good to talk. We haven't really had a chance since Italy."

"No Maya tonight?"

"She left about 4:00, said she was going to Sam's to study, but didn't mention if she'd be home for dinner. Actually, Jonathan, I'm worried about her. Have you noticed anything different? Since Italy she seems, I don't know, sort of closed down."

He took a bite of the enchilada. "Italy was very hard. Seeing her mother's grave, and hearing what my brother-in-law went through, was tough for both of us. It made it real, you know?"

She tried to picture them there, seeing Sophia's grave for the first time. Tears came to her eyes unbidden, and she looked down at her food, blinking them away. Here she was thinking about romance with a man who had lived through the worst nine months of his life. She cleared her throat. "I'm really sorry, Jonathan. Of course it was hard. I'm sure that's what's bothering her."

"Nothing to be sorry about. It was healing in a way too. Like…" He thought for a time, and she held her breath hoping he'd keep talking. "It was like Sophia's death became permanent. And once I understood that, I knew we could make it. I knew for the first time that life would go on. I guess I'd been living in suspended animation since it all happened."

She had no words for that and just nodded. "How did Maya do with it all?"

Again, he looked reflective. "I think it was good for her too. For us together. It brought us closer, I think. But maybe I haven't been paying attention. You think there's something wrong?"

She knew she had to tread lightly, talking to parents about their children is a tricky thing. Parents often take any negative comment about their kids as a personal insult. "I'm not sure. She seems to do her studies, but she doesn't seem excited about them anymore. She spends a lot of time with Sam. Don't get me wrong, I like Sam, but it's almost like she doesn't want to be home anymore." She shut her mouth. There was more she could say but she waited to hear his response.

"I guess I need to pay more attention. Now that you mention it, I haven't seen her much since we got home. I'm sure she's fine. She's such a strong girl, so much like her mother. But I'll check on her soon."

Ashley felt a weight had been lifted off her shoulders. Maya would be looked after by the one person who had any say over her, her father. What she didn't share was her fear that Maya was over-connected to Sam. Whenever she saw them together, Maya was hanging on him, and Sam, for his part, seemed overwhelmed. She hoped Maya wasn't smothering him.

"Ashley," Jonathan said, snapping her out of her pondering. He reached across the table and squeezed her hand sending tingles up her arm. "Thanks for bringing it up. I need you to be honest with me about these things. I'm not always the most perceptive man in the world."

She smiled. He sure wasn't. If he was, he'd know the shock that went through her whole body at his touch. She was falling pretty hard for him and he had no clue. Maybe now was the time. "Johnathan…"

The front door opened, and Maya came in heading straight for the stairs.

"Maya," Jonathan called.

The girl stopped in her tracks. "Yeah?"

"Ashley made enchiladas, they're delicious. You want some?"

Maya didn't even come into the dining room. "No thanks, I ate at Sam's. Gonna study." She bounded up the stairs before anything else could be said.

Jonathan and Ashley exchanged a look. He nodded and Ashley knew he felt it too. There was something not quite right here.

"Excuse me," he said, pushing himself back from the table and following Maya up the stairs.

Ashley hoped this conversation would go well. She left his plate but started to clean up, covering the rest of the enchiladas and rinsing the plates for the dishwasher. When Jonathan came back down, he didn't look happy. He stopped at the table to pick up his plate.

"How'd it go?" she asked.

He shook his head. "Couldn't get much out of her. It's like she's angry about something but doesn't want to talk. I think I'll take this into my room and watch the game." He grabbed his plate and headed for his bedroom.

Ashley shook her head. Anger was a natural response to grief, that made sense, and there was no timeline for grieving. Jonathan thought Maya was like her mother, but right now, she was a carbon copy of her old man, pulling into a hard shell.

CHAPTER FIFTY-EIGHT

Maya

October 17, 2020

I am studying for finals in the living room . . . well, trying to. My mind is bouncing like a bungee jumper. School is much harder than I expected, and online learning takes the fun out of it. But I'm determined to ace my classes.

I got off to a rocky start and have to make up for it. Dad and I had a talk that sort of woke me up. I realized I'd better get to it. I don't want to let him, or Mom, down.

Dad is at work and Ashley's in her room taking tests for her classes. It's a chilly day, and I'm glad to be inside. Reno is having an extended fall this year. Usually, the trees turn colors, shortly followed by a freeze, and the leaves all drop to the ground. This year they are stunning. Many of the trees I can see from my front window are bright gold and red. It would be a great day for a walk if I didn't have other things on my mind.

A knock at the front door pulls me back to the room and pisses me off. It seems like everything irritates me lately. Nobody comes to the door these days. It's probably a political pollster . . . who else would be knocking today? We aren't in total lockdown, but almost, so it's that, or Grandma LaRue, and I don't have time to visit. I slog to the door dragging the blanket I'd wrapped around my shoulders behind me.

Opening it a crack, I see it's Sam standing on the porch looking like a lost kitten. It doesn't help my irritation. I'm not ready to talk to him.

He looks at me with eyes full of hope. "Hi."

"Hi."

"Can I come in?"

"I'm studying." I hope he'll take the hint, but he just stands there looking at me.

"Please, Maya. I won't stay long. You're not returning my texts or calls, and I don't know what I did wrong."

I open the door. Well, I guess this conversation is going to happen, ready or not. I lead him to the couch, where we sit stiffly next to each other. I don't know how to start. Finally, he says, "Are you mad at..."

"No," I say too quickly. The truth is, I'm not mad at him. I'm just mad. I take a breath, but before I can go on, he rushes me.

"I thought we were good after you came back from Italy. I mean, of course, you are sad, and then school started, and we've been busy, but for a while there . . . you were over all the time. But now it feels like something else. Like you're avoiding me. Please, tell me what's going on." He sits very still like he's holding his breath.

I turn to face him. "Sam, it's my period."

"Your period? You don't feel good because of your period. PMS? Cramps? Depre...?" I can tell he is trying really hard.

"No," I interrupt. "I haven't had one. It's late."

His eyes go from confusion to understanding and get very large. "How late?"

"Two weeks."

"But you got that IUD."

"I did." Then I can't help it. My eyes fill with the tears I'd been holding in for the last two weeks. We had such a fun reunion after I got back from Italy. Then I felt so bad, like everything good has been sucked out of the world. Now this. What a roller coaster. "I haven't told anyone." All of the fear comes rushing out. I am sobbing, and he's holding me. And it feels good to be held. I've kept all this to myself for two weeks, trying to think about what to do. *It was the very thing I promised Dad would not happen. The very thing I do not want. I need my mother.*

"Oh, Maya." Sam kisses my hair. "I thought you were breaking up with me. How could you not tell me? You must be so scared."

"I am, was. I wanted time, you know, to decide what to do."

"But I could have helped. I'm involved, you know. If you're . . . pregnant. It's both our problem, or opportunity, right?"

I sit thinking as questions pile up around me. *Is it "both of our" decision? We're so young. Do I want this to waylay my future? Do I want the responsibility of a baby, like Mom and Dad chose when I came along unexpectedly? Do I want to make this decision by myself, or with Sam?*

Sam takes my hand in his. "Of course, it's your decision. Your body. It's just that I want you to know I'm here for you all the way . . . either way. And I'd love to be married to you. I can't see my future with anyone but you. So, if that is what you want, I'll be glad to, you know, step up."

Step up, the words hit me wrong. Guys don't really get it, do they? Still, I sit looking at his lovely, earnest face. *Is that what I want? Or does it just feel good to know it's an option?* I shake my head, squeezing his hand. "I just need time to think. But thank you."

CHAPTER FIFTY-NINE

La Rue

October 2020

LaRue had not heard from Ian, and it had been two weeks since they canvassed the neighborhood. That was a great day, with his goodhearted jesting to make even the door slams less painful. She thought for sure he'd be calling to ask her out, but so far, nothing. She sat on her couch now, remembering that day as she stroked the sleeping cat in her lap.

She'd spent the last two weeks running different scenarios. *Has he forgotten me? Was I wrong to assume there was something between us? Was it all in my mind? Or maybe he'd been dating someone and has to decide between us before he can call? He hadn't mentioned anyone.*

Her cell phone resting on the coffee table jangled causing her to jump.

"Hello," she said hesitantly as his name came up.

"LaRue." His cheerful voice boomed over the phone as if he'd seen her yesterday. "It's Ian . . . from canvassing. How are you?"

"I'm good, Ian. How are you?" She didn't try to keep the coolness from her voice.

"Look, I'm sorry for taking so long to call. One of the grandkids had a scare with the covid, and I needed to wait two weeks to be sure I wasn't infected."

Anger ran through her. "There's this thing called a phone, you know."

"I know and I'm sorry. I also had to sort through some feelings about my late wife. Do you think you could forgive me?"

LaRue relaxed. Well, there wasn't another woman, not a living one anyway. And, she'd had to sort through ten years of feelings herself before she'd decided to date. She needed to cut the guy some slack.

"Of course, Ian. So, did you come to any conclusions?"

"Will you have lunch with me? I'd like to include you in my bubble, but I wanted to make sure it was safe."

That statement took her aback, include her in his bubble? Wasn't that moving from zero to fifty? "I don't know about the bubble, but I'd be glad to go for lunch." She stroked Hershey's fur and enjoyed the loud purr of his response, which sounded like a tea kettle boiling. Petting him helped calm her racing heart.

Ian was quiet for a moment, had she offended him? If he offended that easily, she'd prefer to know now.

"Makes sense," he finally said. "I tend to get ahead of myself. How about I pick you up in an hour?"

LaRue laughed. She guessed this was a man who went after what he wanted. It felt good to be pursued, but she was not going to be rushed. "An hour it is."

Lunch was fast food, as the restaurants were still mostly closed, and they ate in his car again. She didn't mind the casual food at all, and it said something good about him that he didn't mind their eating greasy hamburgers and fries in his nice car. She wasn't sure what it said, but Walter's constant insistence that his car stay pristine had always bugged her.

Some restaurants were open at 25 percent capacity, but she would not have ventured into one. The smart ones had figured out how to do outdoor seating. She wondered how many small businesses would still be standing when this ended. They happily spent the whole lunch hour talking about the mess of Trump's presidency and his mishandling of the pandemic. It felt good to have someone to rant with in person.

The next day they had dinner at his house, a lovely duplex right on the river. "Come in, my bonnie lass," he greeted her at the door.

She brought a dessert of double fudge frosted brownies which seemed to make him very happy.

"Let me show you around." It was a nice, well-appointed condominium with a large sitting area and two bedrooms decorated in muted colors. She wondered if the décor was his choice or his wife's. The kitchen was small for her taste, but the place was in good condition.

In the living room, he lifted a framed picture of his late wife and showed it to her. She was a pleasant-looking woman with red hair and a lot of freckles. "She has a kind face," said LaRue.

"Aye, she did. I wonder, at your place, do you have pictures of Walter about?"

Of course she did, she had several. She had never thought to take them down. Would this be a problem for him? "I do." She watched his face to see how he'd take it..

"I'm glad. These people were with us a long time and I'd like to be able to remember them, not tip-toe around them like uncomfortable ghosts when I'm dating someone."

That made LaRue smile, and they agreed that losing a long-term spouse did not mean you had to remove all traces of them. She was glad there was no jealousy there. Walter was an important part of her life and always would be. Also, Ian said they were *dating*.

About a week later, Ian took her to meet his daughter, Fiona. She felt embarrassed by the butterflies in her stomach as they pulled up to his daughter's house. The home was a modest starter, but the grass was well-kept. *Aren't I too old for butterflies?* But she knew how important this woman was to Ian. He'd talked about her and his son Trevor, a lot. What if they didn't like her? Dad bringing home a new woman after the death of a beloved mother would be difficult for them.

She held her breath as Ian knocked. A petite red-head opened the door. "Da. And you must be LaRue. I've heard a lot about you. Please come in." Two girls LaRue knew were a raven haired eight year old and a blonde nine year old, mobbed their grandfather as they entered. It was good to see Ian was well-loved by his grandchildren. Kids and grandkids could tell you a lot about a person's character. The girls dragged Ian into the living room to play. She stood watching and he looked at her as if helpless to untangle himself.

Fiona took her arm and led her into the kitchen where she was preparing a tray with some tea and cookies. "I'm sorry about that. Saoirse and Evanna love their Papa." Fiona turned to her, "You know, you're the first woman he's brought around since my mom died."

"Oh," was all she could think to say.

"He seems quite smitten." Fiona placed cookies and donut holes on the tray while LaRue stood by the counter watching. Her face was tight, as if she wasn't quite sure about LaRue. "He speaks quite highly of you."

Was she supposed to reply? "He's a charming man, and he obviously adores you and the girls."

Fiona smiled. "That he is. And a good judge of character, so I want you to know that if he trusts you, I trust you." The words felt a bit forced.

"Trust me?" LaRue enjoyed Fiona's no-nonsense attitude, but she could tell the woman was appraising her somehow. What was it she wanted to know?

"Yes, I think he'd spot a gold digger."

LaRue laughed. "I did a bit of dating online before I met your dad. It was awful. I did meet one of those." She shivered, remembering the slimy way she'd felt after Hank asked so many questions about her finances. "I can assure you I own my own home and my husband left me a good pension. No need to worry that I'm after your dad's money."

Fiona's shoulders lowered a notch. She must have been worried about her dad, but LaRue could tell she'd passed at least one test. The rest of the visit was delightful.

Chapter Sixty

Maya

October 23, 2020

It's a blustery fall day, which always makes me think of *Winnie the Pooh* and my mom. She and I watched those animated cartoons—the classic ones, not the new ones—and snuggled together on the couch. I'm just leaving my lab when, who should I see, but Sam? He's been showing up, in one way or another, every day since our talk.

"Hello, sunshine." He greets me with a grin.

That makes me laugh and he takes my hand as we start toward the neighborhood. It's true I'm not as grouchy as I was, but I'm hardly a ray of sunshine. He hands me a bag, but I already know what's in it. Every day he brings me two things: some form of chocolate, and a pregnancy test. Every day the test is negative, and the chocolate is welcome.

"What are you doing here? Don't you have your next class soon?" Sam's been doing his TMCC classes online, but he's working hard and determined to get good grades so he can transfer to UNR in two years so we'll be on the same campus . . . if they ever open.

"We had a test today. We could log in any time after midnight to take it, so I already did it."

"How did it go?"

"Aced it." That's one cool thing about some of these online tests, they tell you right away how you did.

"Hey, aren't you going to see what I brought you?"

"I'm pretty sure I know what it is." I peek into the bag. The test was there but the chocolate *du jour* was a surprise. "Reese's."

"You can share half of it and still have a whole."

He raised his eyebrows at me with a puppy dog face, so I stopped to open the candy and give him half. "I'm pretty sure you got the wrong jingle there, buddy, but I'll still share."

"Melts in your mouth and not in your hands?" he says as he removes the thin brown wrapper from the chocolatey, peanut-buttery deliciousness and pops the whole thing in his mouth.

"Not even close. And I can't believe you just did that."

"What?" He mumbles around the glob in his mouth.

"I like to eat the edges first, then the bottom, then the chocolatey top." I take a nibble, enjoying the sweetness.

He shakes his head at me, swallowing. "So, have you had any thoughts about the, you know, possible progeny?"

I know he's trying to be funny, but the word progeny doesn't help. I was a surprise baby for my parents—what if they'd decided not to keep me? I mean I understand, but also, I wouldn't be here. "No."

We walk a while in silence, then I realize how kind and supportive Sam is being. "I'm going to call the

women's center when I get home and see about getting a blood test, just to be sure. Then I can relax."

He takes my hand and we head up the hill. "That
sounds like a good idea."

CHAPTER SIXTY-ONE

LaRue

October 2020

LaRue pulled out her white lace tablecloth and spread it over the small table in her kitchen. It had been a long time since she'd set a nice table. Since she usually ate in front of the TV on a tray. She opened the hutch and pulled out her Moss Rose china. They'd need a rinse. Why did she feel nervous? She'd been dating Ian for two months, and she enjoyed being with him immensely.

"I know why I'm nervous, Walter. What if he wants to, you know, stay over?"

Why am I asking my late husband for sex advice? It had just been so long since she'd had to think about it. What did she know about sex these days? Ashley had given her the "no glove, no love" lecture, which she explained meant that you had to use a rubber to guard against sexual diseases. But she'd never had an STD, and hadn't been with anyone since Walter. She wondered about Ian. Could he say the same? Could a man his age even perform sexually? Would he want to?

Ashley had also told her to shave her legs, which she refused to do. What hair she had left on her legs was very soft. *Why is that necessary? It all seems so complicated.*

What she did know about was food. She made a delicious apple-walnut salad, a warm mushroom soup, and for the entree, pork chops, mashed potatoes, and gravy, with some homemade applesauce. And for dessert, if there was room for dessert, one of her famous chocolate fudge pies. She lit the candles just as the knock came at the door.

She took off her apron and laid it on the counter before going to the door, Hershey at her heels. Hershey seemed to know when it was Ian. Damn cat actually liked him!

LaRue opened the door, and there he was, neat and clean, looking handsome in his argyle sweater over black slacks and holding a beautiful bouquet of red roses. Hershey immediately twined around his ankles. "Come in, come in. Those are beautiful. Careful of the cat."

She led him in and shut the door against the late October chill.

"You look wonderful." He smiled at her and kissed her cheek. "That sweater matches your eyes perfectly." He leaned down to pet Hershey who set to purring like a wanton woman. The cat had never taken to anyone as he had to Ian, not even Maya.

"Thank you," she said, taking the flowers and glad she'd opted for the soft blue cashmere sweater set she'd bought on impulse two weeks ago online. She inhaled a deep breath of the roses before heading to the kitchen for a vase.

He followed behind, stopping to examine the table. "What is that titillating smell?"

"Oh, you'll just have to see." LaRue gestured to the table. "I've made all my favorites." They were actually Walter's favorites, but she didn't want to tell Ian that.

"Love, you've outdone yourself; this table is a stunner."

His Irish lilt was so attractive, and he complimented her so often it almost felt unreal and when he called her *Love*, she felt all fluttery, like a hummingbird had taken residence in her heart. Walter had been much less effusive. She collected the salad and soup plates off the table for the first course. "I haven't had a chance to entertain in a long time. It was fun to pull out the good dishes." They'd mostly eaten out or had dinner at his house; this was her first time cooking for him. He was a good cook, himself, if not creative.

She placed the food on the plates and brought them to the table, then sat across from him. His eyes danced in the candlelight. He lifted his glass of red wine toward her. "To the chef."

She laughed and clinked his glass, watching with joy as he dug into the food, making appreciative noises and complementing each dish. Her heart felt warm and happy in a way it hadn't in so long. She relaxed, and they began a deep conversation about life and politics and the crazy presidential debates. She'd missed this companionship more than any other part of marriage, having someone to talk with about the little things at the end of the day.

After dinner, they took their pie and coffee into the living room. "Music or Netflix?" she asked as he settled onto the couch.

"Music," he said. She felt a stirring in her lower regions, which had been quiet for a long time.

"I know you have a much nicer music system than I do, but I hope you don't mind this one." This one was a music streaming service Maya had set up for her with two small speakers and her phone. She'd paid for the service to eliminate the obnoxious commercials on the free version. She put John Legend in as her category and thought that might set a good mood. Joining him on the couch, she sipped her decaf as he scraped the last of the pie from his plate.

"This is like eating fudge."

She loved a man who could eat. "That's why I just gave you a small slice. It's a recipe from my southern grandmother—very rich. I'll let you take the rest over to Fiona and the girls, or I'll eat the whole thing."

He nodded. "But not before I drop off a slice or two at my place. You know, LaRue, I love this house. It's a cozy little nest you have here. Don't get me wrong. I like my condo by the river. I enjoy walking by the river, but it's just not the same as a home, and I miss having a backyard to putter around in."

"Yes," she sighed happily. "There's just something healing about getting your fingers in the dirt." She wondered where he was going with this. *Is he hinting that he'd like to move in with me?* What would that be like? The thought gave her quite a thrill . . . it also caused her to pause. She'd enjoyed her independence since Walter died. No one to take care of. Only her needs to consider. To have a man around again would be an adjustment . . . but also kind of nice. Someone to help with the house when things broke. Someone to talk to.

She put her empty coffee cup down next to her untouched pie, too full to eat. He slipped his arm around her shoulders, pulled her close, and kissed her gently on the lips. She enjoyed his kisses, they made her feel young again. And tonight he tasted like chocolate mocha.

"LaRue," he said, pulling back to look into her eyes. "We're not getting any younger, and we both know that life can be cut off at any minute."

Her heart started racing. Was he going to ask her to marry him? To move in together. Where was this going?

"I know it might be kind of forward but, if it's okay with you, I have my overnight bag in the car."

He waited for her to process his statement. Was it okay with her? She smiled; damn right it was. "That would be lovely," she said.

CHAPTER SIXTY-TWO

Ashley

October 2020

Ashley curled up on the Lazy Boy chair in her room, coffee in hand, and logged onto Zoom. After her visit home, she'd taken her mom's advice and reached out to a girlfriend. Her mom told her before she left, "Ash, you need to get some girlfriends. We women need a tribe. And try to find some your age, not just a 75-year-old and a 17-year-old, okay?"

"Okay, Mom," she assured her. But the thing was, she didn't have any girlfriends. Mark had made sure of that, and the friends she'd made at work were gone with the job.

The only one she knew in town, who she felt she could reach out to, was Tess. She'd met Tess on Parker's happy hour Zooms, back when they were dating. She liked the curly-headed woman immediately, so she ate humble pie and sent a text to Parker to ask for Tess's number. He was not overly warm toward her, but he did send her the number. Ashley texted Tess quickly, before she could chicken out. The woman seemed happy to reconnect and they'd been texting ever since. Today was their first Zoom visit.

Tess's happy face lit up the screen. "Ashley. It's so good to see you. Thank you so much for taking the initiative."

Ashley breathed out. This was good for her. Her mom was right. "Thanks for saying yes. It's kind of lonely during this pandemic."

"That's the understatement of the world. At least you have people to live with. Being single during the pandemic is hard, and people always say insensitive things like, 'at least I'm not alone. I'd die if I had to do this alone,' like I'm not sitting right there."

Ashley winced. "I'm so sorry. That's horrible." She wondered if she'd said anything like that to anyone. "But at least you have your happy hours."

Tess lifted her shoulders. "Sometimes. It hasn't been very consistent with, you know, Parker and Cassandra being on and off all the time. Plus, Cheryl's pregnancy has worn her out. She's due next month—November 8th, I think."

"Wow, she must be getting big."

"She is, but you know, she's one of those gals who looks cute pregnant. I'd probably look like a barn."

They laughed. *This isn't so hard,* thought Ashley. She shouldn't have worried; Tess was one of those happy extroverts who could carry a conversation all by herself.

"I know it's early, but my family decided to buy our Christmas presents from small and local businesses this year because everyone is struggling. I've found my new thrill, shopping on Etsy."

Ashley laughed. "I love Etsy." Etsy was the online place to buy homemade crafts and things. "Do you know what I was thinking about? Usually, December is super busy and stressful, all these end of the year parties, and my niece's classes' holiday presentations, and things. This year is going to be *much* quieter. I think I might like it. But Christmas is going to be weird. I don't know if I'll go home. I doubt my brother and the girls will even be there. What will you be doing?"

"I'm not sure yet." Tess drank from her mug. "I know it will be small, probably just my mom and me. I doubt we'll even have trick-or-treaters for Halloween, and it will probably just be Mom and me for Thanksgiving too."

"True," agreed Ashley. "It's a year for low-key holidays."

"Yeah, remind me of that next year if the world is back to normal, will you? I might want to say no to some parties and things."

"Do you think it will ever be back to normal? It seems like things keep getting worse." Ashley's mind flew back over recent events. The virus was worse locally; California had shut down again; and politically, things were really chaotic.

"I have no idea. But they are working on a vaccine. I'm hoping for that."

"Me too." Ashley took a sip of her coffee. She hated to ask, but she was curious. "So, how are Parker and Cassandra? *On* again, or *off* again?"

"Oh, you know." Tess laughed. "I've lost track. But tell me more about that guy you texted me about. Any movement on that hunk you're caged with? Has he noticed you yet?"

Ashley felt a thrill running up her spine. "Jonathan? Well, maybe…"

"What do you mean, *maybe?* Tell all."

"I don't know. It's just that sometimes I see him looking at me, ya know, I glance up at dinner, and he's looking at me. Or like when he takes my hand to help me out of the truck, it seems like he holds it a bit too long."

"Ooh, how very Jane Austen."

Ashley smiled. "I don't know, maybe I'm just making it up. Wishful thinking and all."

"Oh no. You've got to trust your intuition on this. You said he came back from Italy different, right?"

"It sure seems like it. He's, I don't know, softer somehow. He laughs more, and he isn't always hiding in his room. He talks more. I really like having him around now."

"And what about Maya? Has she noticed?"

"Hmm, I think maybe she's noticed but hasn't said anything. The other night at dinner, she looked back and forth between her dad and me several times. She raised her eyebrows at me and smiled. I know I blushed like a teenager. But that was all." She sipped her coffee. "She seems really distracted lately. I guess she's busy with school."

"Well, are you going to say anything, to Jonathan, I mean?"

"I don't know. Do you think I should?"

Tess pulled on a curl; it seemed to indicate she was thinking. "Well, why not?"

Another tingle ran up Ashley's spine. *Why not?* She'd have to think about that.

CHAPTER SIXTY-THREE

Maya

October 31, 2020

I am putting the final touches on my cat make-up when there's a knock at my bedroom door. "Come in," I yell, drawing the last whisker on my cheek.

Dad pokes his head in. "Don't you look cute."

I have to agree. I am wearing a black leotard and leggings, cat ears, and cat makeup. A black tail completes the outfit. "Sam and I are going to hand out candy. He made a way to get the candy into the kid's baskets from six feet away with a PVC pipe."

"That's creative." Dad comes all the way in and shuts the door, which is kind of odd. Then he sits on my bed. Even odder. Does he have suspicions about my non-existent period? I keep taking pregnancy tests and they all come up negative, but still, no period. The clinic can't get me in till next month for a checkup because . . . covid. But how would Dad know any of that? I haven't even told Ashley.

I turn my vanity chair around to face him. He looks odd, like nervous.

"I'm not sure how to say this," he begins.

My mind dashes around like a ping-pong ball: *We're going to lose the house. Someone has died. We're moving...* I don't say anything. I just wait.

"Going to Italy was really helpful for me." He nods.

I nod back. It was good for me too, and he has seemed much lighter since we got back. Like maybe he felt guilty, as if he could have prevented Mom's death somehow. But being in Italy and seeing the devastation made him realize there was nothing he could have done to save her. I don't know what to say so I keep quiet. He fidgets and takes a deep breath like he's bracing himself.

"Pumpkin, I want you to know that you are the most important thing in my life," he looks at his shoes. *Is he going to tell me he's dying?*

"Dad, what is it? You're starting to freak me out."

He grins then, and his face changes, taking about ten years off his age. "It's Ashley."

Ashley? That stumps me. *Is he mad at her? Does he want her to move out?* "What about her?"

And then he speaks in a rush without even taking a breath. "I wondered how you would feel if I asked her out. I mean I don't have to if you think it's too soon. Or if you think it's weird, or if you think I'm too old, or it would be wrong, since she lives here and technically works for me. Or..."

Then it's like he runs out of steam and just stares at me like a little lost boy. *Ashley. I knew something was going on there. I caught them glancing at each other at dinner. Hmm. How do I feel about that? Kind of sad. If Dad dates Ashley, it means Mom isn't coming back. I know Mom isn't coming back, but it makes it really real. And Ashley is my friend. Would it be weird if she was dating Dad? But he has a right to be happy; so does she. I'm happy with Sam. Everyone needs someone.*

I guess I'm taking too long to answer. Dad starts to get up. "You probably need some time to think about it. It's okay. I don't need an answer right now. Just let me know when you've thought about it. I'm okay if the answer is no, totally okay. As I said, you are the most important thing to me."

He starts toward my door and suddenly I know. *I love Ashley and I love Dad. If it works out between them it would be great. We could be a family again. A real family.* "Dad," I say before he leaves. I notice his shoulders are slightly slumped.

He turns to me slowly.

"I'd love it if you dated Ashley."

His face transforms into a wide grin and he stands straighter. "Really? You'd be okay with that? But what if she's not interested?"

Now, he looks like a little boy again. This is like watching my dad morph through every possible emotion. My stoic father is acting like a teenager. He's acting like me. *Yikes!* "Dad, I think we are all close enough and she is honest enough that if she isn't interested, she'll tell you, but it won't ruin what we have. Don't you think that's true?"

He grins again, releasing a breath. "I think so."
Then he steps back to me and hugs me. I try not to get
cat makeup on his shirt. When he pulls back his eyes
are watery, and he takes another deep breath. "I can't
believe how nervous I am." He laughs.

"Dad, you'll be fine. Just do it. Soon, ya know, carpe
diem and all that."

"Great," he chuckles. "Now I'm getting dating advice from my teenage daughter."

I grin at him as he turns to the door. It's kind of
weird but good too. It feels right.

CHAPTER SIXTY-FOUR

LaRue

November 2020

LaRue and the girls sat in her living room enjoying the crackling fire and a glass of wine. There was a beautiful nip to the fall air and LaRue was eager for the smell of wood smoke.

"So…" began Betty, "…how are you and Ian getting along?"

"Oh, I don't know." LaRue didn't really want to talk about Ian, she'd been feeling all sorts of things lately and not all of them made sense.

"You don't know?" said Jackie, sitting up suddenly. "You two are practically inseparable. And didn't you say he'd spent the night? How did that go?"

"It went fine. You know, a bit of a fumble at first but we figured it out."

Betty sat down her wine as if to make a point. "Then what's the problem?"

LaRue looked at her friends, she was glad they'd all agreed to be in the same bubble, and they were good to her, kind, and loving, but how did she explain this? "He makes a lot of jokes."

Jackie raised an eyebrow. "You said you liked his sense of humor."

"I do, most of the time. But he can be loud. He keeps talking about the house, hinting that he'd like to move in. And you know me. It's a small house, and I'm used to quiet."

"Oh." Jackie nodded and sat back on the couch sipping her wine. "That makes sense. It sounds like he's ready to take things to the next level and you're not sure you are."

LaRue thought about that. She did love Ian, and had told him so. She did want to take things to the next level, whatever that meant. "There's something I've never told you two."

"What?" Betty's eyes grew large.

"It's a bit embarrassing, but for the last eleven years, since Walter died, I've been talking to him. Out loud." She held her breath, waiting for them to ask if she'd lost her mind.

Instead, her two friends looked at each other, then at her. Betty licked her lips. "That's no secret, sweetie. We've all heard you talk to Walter."

"You have?" Heat flushed LaRue's face. "I didn't know that."

"We've always thought it was sweet," Jackie hurried to say.

LaRue gulped. "But what if I do it around Ian? I'm terrified I will, and I'm sure it won't make him feel good to know I've had an ongoing relationship with my late husband for the last ten years."

"Look," said Jackie pointing a finger. "You will have an 'ongoing relationship' with Walter for the rest of your life. It will just change now. Ian will slowly become the one you talk to. He'll take Walter's place in the day-to-day."

Betty nodded. "I agree. And I think you need to tell him about it. He'll understand, if anyone will. He's lost a wife."

"You really think so?" Her friends nodded; they seemed so sure. "I almost feel like I need to break up with Walter to really date Ian. I mean, when we had sex, it seemed like a threesome."

Her friends burst into laughter and LaRue had to join them. "Well, not a threesome in a sexual way, but like Walter was hovering."

"You said you felt Walter approved of Ian, right?" asked Jackie.

"Yes, I really think he does."

Betty's eyes lit up. "I know what you need—a ritual."

"What?" LaRue noticed Hershey had entered the room. She patted her lap, so he jumped up. He was such a comfort. "Like an exorcism?

Betty laughed. "No. Pastor Claire is always talking about the importance of ritual to mark important events. Like you could pack away some of Walter's things to make the house less Walter-y."

"Oh," agreed Jackie. "And you could write Walter a letter to tell him it's time to move on, and burn it, or bury it, or something."

LaRue was getting excited. "This sounds like it might help."

LaRue knelt on the foam pad in her garden where she'd cleared a patch of land to plant bulbs for the spring. She took the letter she'd written Walter and read it out loud. She was glad there was no one around to hear her.

My Dearest,

It has been eleven years now since you've been gone and not a day goes by that I don't think of you and miss you. But as you know, it's time for me to make room for a new man in my life. You will still be with me always, but now it's time for Ian to take first place.

A tear slid down LaRue's cheek and she brushed it away with the back of her garden glove.

He's a good man. I know you'd approve. He's different from you, but then, I've changed a lot since we were together. I go to a different church, I have different friends . . . and this pandemic- it changes people.

I am putting in a circle of lavender tulips, which are your favorite. I don't know if I need permission to move on or it's just that I seem to need to let you go. Either way, I'm asking for your help. Help me let go of you. Help me love Ian freely and without reserve. He deserves that. And I guess I do too.

Forever my first love,

LaRue (aka Honey Bunny)

She folded the paper into a small square and tucked it into the hole she'd dug, dropping a bulb in on top of it. Lovingly she removed her glove and brushed in fresh dirt.

CHAPTER SIXTY-FIVE

Ashley

November 2020

Ashley came down the stairs ready to celebrate. She'd just passed her first advanced pharmacology test. Was anyone home to rejoice with her? Jonathan was in the kitchen and looked up as she entered.

"How did it go?"

"I aced it." She did a little dance around the living room.

"We should celebrate. Want to go to Starbucks?"

"Don't have to ask me twice." She grabbed her sweater off the hook by the door before realizing that

Jonathan had never asked her to go anywhere alone with him. Except, of course, when she was nursing him back to health from covid, and she made him take walks with her every day, but that was at her insistence. The thought made her breath catch. *It's just coffee.* She coached herself. *He's just being nice to celebrate with me.*

He came over to get his jacket and then pulled open the door with a sweeping gesture for her to go out first. She tried not to read anything into that either, but when he raced ahead of her to the passenger side of his truck and opened that door. Her nerve endings started to spark. *Is this happening?*

He jumped into the driver's side of the truck and started the engine without looking at her. She stared at her fingers, unsure of what to say as he backed out of the driveway. "What are your plans for the rest of the day?" he asked.

"I have no plans. I need a break from studying."

"Great," he said, still not looking at her. "My brother and his family are finally back from New York. Maybe after we get coffee we can stop by and say hi."

"Uh, okay."

"Don't worry. They had to get negative covid tests to even get on the airplane home."

"Oh, cool." She'd just let him think it was covid she was worried about and not the fact that he wanted to introduce her to his family. The drive to Starbucks was short, and soon they were in line to order in the drive-through.

"I realize I have no idea what you like." He turned to her, smiling.

Tension around his eyes made her wonder if he was nervous too. *Is he going to ask me to move out? Does he need to talk about Maya, who's been acting weird since school started? Maybe that's why he suddenly wants to be with me alone.*

"I'd like a Caramel Macchiato, please."

He pulled up to the speaker and asked for a Black coffee for himself and a Caramel Macchiato for her.

"What size?" came over the speaker.

He glanced at her with raised eyebrows.

"Grande," she said, and he repeated it toward the speaker. They pulled forward.

"What the heck is a Caramel Macchiato?"

She relaxed a bit. "Steamed milk, espresso, and vanilla syrup."

"Uh, sounds like candy in a cup," he joked.

She was surprised when he pulled the truck into a parking place after getting their drinks at the take-out window. He turned off the engine and unbuckled his seatbelt, put his drink on the dash, and turned to face her.

She placed her drink in the cup holder and braced herself. This could be good; this could be bad. She waited, then took a sip of her coffee.

"You know that trip to Italy was good for me," he began, a red flush creeping up his neck, the only indication that this was hard for him.

"I've noticed you seem … happier."

"Yeah. I feel kind of, uh, unstuck. And that's what I want to talk to you about. But it's tricky because I don't want to damage our friendship in any way."

He got quiet and looked down, and Ashley knew, for a man of few words, this was a lot for him. "Jonathan, there is nothing you could say to me that would damage our friendship. If you need me to move out or anything, I completely understand."

His head jerked up, his eyes wide. "No. I mean, that's not it at all—the opposite actually. I just . . . well, I'd like it if we could go out, but if you're not interested, I'm afraid to hurt our friendship. You mean a lot to Maya and...to me." He fell silent again.

He wanted to date her? She let that sink in. A flush settled over her body like glitter, and she felt a grin she couldn't suppress. But Maya suddenly came between them as if she were a physical presence in the car. "Um, what would Maya think?"

He looked down, grinning. "I asked her first. She's good with it, if you are."

She unbuckled her seatbelt, put her coffee next to his, and moved closer to him. Placing her hand carefully on his knee, she looked into his handsome face. He stiffened as if she was preparing to reject him.

"Jonathan, I'd be pleased and proud to date you. You are one of the kindest, hardest-working men I have ever met. And the way you are with Maya, it's beautiful." Then she leaned in slowly and placed a light kiss on his lips.

He jerked back in surprise. "Well then." Suddenly he smiled, his body relaxing. "Let's try that again." He gently took her face in his hands and gazed into her eyes. Tilting his head as he leaned in.

Her heart hammered like a drum as he neared. He smelled of soap and mint. His lips met hers. They were warm and soft, then insistent. She felt a rush of warmth flood her body as he pressed his kiss more deeply. She had waited a long time for this kiss, and it was worth the wait.

CHAPTER SIXTY-SIX

Dresses

December 2020

LaRue

"Ian, can you zip me up?"

"Of course, my beauty." Ian came up behind LaRue. They were in her bedroom as she stood in front of the mirror atop her dresser. The dress was beautiful, he'd helped her pick it out, saying the forest green reminded him of Ireland. He zipped the dress and then placed a kiss on her neck, sending shivers down her back. How had she been this lucky to find two men in her lifetime who loved her so well? It had all happened fast, but as she knew, life was unpredictable, and you had to live it while you could.

"Are you nervous?" he asked.

"Not really. Maybe a little." She turned to face him. "Today will change everything. It will be official." She grinned.

He pulled her into a warm hug, "Well, I'm ready for that, my lass. Our future together starts with a wedding. Quite appropriate, I'd say." He held her shoulders and kissed her.

Maya

I tap on Ashley's door, feeling nervous. Today is the day, and I want it to be perfect.

"Come in."

I open the door. Ashley is sitting in front of her vanity. She turns to me and gasps. "Maya, you look lovely."

That is exactly the reaction I was hoping for. I step into the room, twirling slowly, so my dress flares out around me. "It's not too tight, is it? I can't seem to stop gaining weight."

"That's only natural. You were much too thin any-way."

I smile at that. "It's true. Can you do up the buttons in the back for me?"

"Of course." Ashley stands. Her make-up looks beautiful, and she has piled her hair up in a loose bun, so the sides hang down in curls around her face.

"You look amazing too. I can't wait to see you in your dress."

Ashley buttons me up and turns me around, grasping my shoulders. "I'm excited for this day, but – are you sure this is what you want? Remember all the options we spoke about."

I remember; how can I not remember? Big decisions, big discussions, big options. "I'm sure. I'm ready."

She pulls me into a hug. "I'm so glad. Now go finish getting ready."

Ashley

Ashley stared at herself in her bedroom mirror. Yep, she was ready. She'd chosen a simple cream-colored dress with an empire waist and pearl bodice, a wreath of flowers in her hair. Since it was Christmastime, they'd gone with creams, reds, and greens.

Her mother stood next to her, beaming. "You look amazing, darling." She wiped a tear from her eyes. "This is some little family you've found."

"I'm so glad to be a part of it, Mom." She squeezed her mother's hand. Thankful her folks had been able to come—negative covid tests were required of all who entered their home today.

There was a tap on the door, and her father poked his head in. "Oh, look at my beautiful women. How lucky I am. It's time. Are we ready?"

Ashley grinned at her father and nodded. He looked dapper in his gray suit. Her mom kissed her cheek and rushed out the door to take her place with the others. Her father held out his arm. The strains of *Ode to Joy* wafted up from downstairs. She smiled up at her father and took his arm.

They stepped down the stairs together. Evergreen swaths wrapped the banister, with shiny red and cream ornaments woven in. Maya and LaRue did a great job. Down below, she saw the small gathering, Sam and his parents, her brother and his family, Jonathan's brother and his wife and children, and LaRue's Ian. In front of the fireplace stood LaRue in green, Maya in red, and Jonathan in gray. When he saw her coming down the stairs, his eyes went wide, and tears coursed down his cheeks. He did not wipe them away. Her heart fluttered in her chest. This, 2020, had been the most challenging year of their lives, and yet there was great joy and newness to it as well. It brought hope that 2021 would be a better year.

CHAPTER SIXTY-SEVEN

Maya

December 19, 2020

What a perfect day. I stand by the fireplace with LaRue on my right and Dad on my left. We are waiting for Ashley to make her entrance. Dad shifts from one foot to the other, nervous and stiff in his new suit.

The house smells like the pine boughs we decorated with and the cinnamon-apple cider that fills the crockpot. The kitchen counter is piled with food just waiting for us after the ceremony. LaRue and her friends outdid themselves.

I look at Sam, who smiles at me. His folks sit next to him on the sofa, wearing masks. It's a cozy group, just right.

I know, to some of the folks in our home, it must seem sudden, especially Dad's brother, Uncle Todd, and his family. It must seem too fast, but they haven't lived through the hell we have. I guess they've gone through their own hell, stuck in New York with Dad's parents. And poor Grandma and Grandpa can't even be here. They gave Dad an ear-chewing, I'm sure. But this is happening, and it is right. When Ashley and Dad realized they were in love, and living under the same roof, they decided a wedding was the way to go. Uncle Todd has his phone out, ready to record the wedding for his folks.

Ashley's friend, Tess, pushes play on her phone. She is wearing a green dress with a red scarf. She got licensed as an officiant in Nevada so she can perform this wedding. Now that's a good friend.

Ode to Joy bursts from the speakers and we all turn to the stairs. Ashley's mother comes quickly down to take her place on a chair up front. Then we see Ashley and her father, and she looks perfect. She wears a simple dress that she had kept hidden from all of us, her hair gently topped with a wreath in small red, green, and cream-colored flowers. LaRue and I wear matching wreaths. I'm loving this Christmassy wedding. Dad sniffs; he's crying. Oh no. That sets me off, and now LaRue is passing me tissues. I hand one to Dad and keep one for myself. I'm pretty sure there's not a dry eye in the house.

Ashley kisses her father at the bottom of the stairs and then comes to stand by Dad. It's a simple ceremony. They want it that way. They repeat lines after Tess, then each recites their vows. I can't take my eyes off Dad. He looks happier than I've seen him in almost a year. So much has happened. I miss my mother. I'd rather have her here than all of this, but I know deeply that since it's not possible, this is the next best thing. I think she'd approve.

And then Dad and Ashley kiss and everyone is cheering and rushing up to hug them. LaRue and I scuttle to the kitchen to get the food unwrapped, and people start to fill their plates.

Sam comes over to hug me. "You look great." He puts his arm around me and draws me close. He whispers in my ear, "Maybe someday it will be ours, but I'm glad it's not today."

"Me too." I smile at him. We were so relieved when I finally got to the doctor, and he told me my period was not coming because of stress. Between school, losing Mom, flying to Italy and back, the graveyard emotions, and all the pandemic stuff, I was turning into a stress ball. He recommended therapy, and I've been meeting with an online therapist ever since. She is awesome. It has helped, and guess what? My period came back; my appetite too.

Dad clinks a spoon on his wine glass, and everyone quiets down. "A toast," he says. He holds his glass in the air. "I'd like to thank the three women who have made today possible. My lovely daughter, who has stood by me through the hardest year of our lives." He nods at me, beaming. I smile back.

"LaRue," he continues, "who has been like a mom and grandma to us during this difficult time. I'm so thankful for you." LaRue grins back at him and blows a kiss back. I remember the scare when she got covid, we were so afraid we would lose her too. I'm glad she's okay.

"And of course," Dad turns to Ashley, who stands next to him holding his hand. "To my bride, who not only nursed me back to health. And, trust me, that was a job nobody would want." People laugh at that. Especially Uncle Todd. "She also nursed my heart back to life when it was badly broken." Ashley grins, and everyone applauds as he kisses her.

I'm not gonna lie. It's going to take some time to get used to watching Dad kiss Ashley. It still feels very weird to me. I also don't know what it will be like to have her as a stepmom and not a friend. She told me, "Nothing has to change between us. You already have a mom. Even if she is gone from this world, she will always be your mom." I appreciate that and I suppose Ashley will stay my friend too.

What a strange year. The memories cycle through my brain: Mom goes to Italy, and she, Nonna, and Nonno get sick and die, even before we really knew what covid-19 was. It all happened so fast, like the world turned upside down overnight. And school was hard back then, and I got beat up the first day, but then I met Sam and life got a little better. Then the pandemic crashed in on us, and we couldn't go to school. Then Dad got sick. I remember feeling so alone when LaRue got sick. And Ashley, who I didn't even really know, started coming to help. Boy, what a mess. Ashley moved in to help us all get through it. What would we have done without her?

There is more glass clinking, and I'm drawn to LaRue, who is tapping her wine glass. "Not to steal your thunder, but since we are all family here, I have an announcement too."

I wonder what it is. Ian has a Leprechaun grin as everyone gives LaRue their attention. "Ian has decided to move in with me, so we'll add one more person to our little family."

Everyone cheers as Ian kisses LaRue's cheek. I head over to hug her. "Congratulations," I say, and hug Ian too. I don't know him well yet, but he seems to have put the blush back into LaRue's cheeks, and I'm glad for her to have someone special to share her life with, especially after that disastrous series of online dates.

"Moving in together, eh? You crazy kids," I tease.

"Yep," says LaRue, beaming. "And Ian's going to add a second story to the house, so we don't kill each other."

We laugh and I hug "Grandma."

"Pictures," yells Tess. "Family first, Jonathan, Ashley, Maya, LaRue, and now we can add Ian. You all come over to the fireplace, please."

We stand together there. A year ago, we were just neighbors. Now, we are a family brought together by a virus. A terrible virus, yes, but also a love virus.

CHAPTER SIXTY-EIGHT

Acknowledgements

The pandemic was hard! Four years after it started, we are still trying to understand the repercussions. As I write this, my husband has covid for the first time; it is not done with us. We lost our dear friend, Mike, and our beloved Dadish, Carl, to this virus. It has changed our lives forever. Some still struggle with long-term covid health issues, and children lost two years of schooling, proms, graduations, and birthday parties.

Yet, some things made it manageable for me.

Love to my pandemic bubble: David, Sarah, Micah, Susie, Norah, and Lemon. Oh yes, and our dog Rosie, who faithfully got us outside every day. I'm so glad we had each other.

And my online critique group who helped me write this book during the pandemic: Sue C. Dugan, Suzanne Morgan Williams, Linda Kay Hardie, and Marie Navarro. And to Sarah DeLacey for a first-read and great feedback.

To my editor Carol Purroy who helped me when I started eleven years ago and edited this book. You make me a better writer. Thank you. And to Bryce Minturn, one of the best young writers who continues to inspire me daily and helps me edit too!

Thanks to my ARC readers! Ransom, Theresa, Diana, Debra, Paul, Lorita, Bridget, Barb, Bryce, Sue, Marie Ann, Francine, Joanne, Laura, Miriam, Glendanne, Lynn, Betty, Teri, Sharon, Tamera, Carol, Ann, Carrie, Linda, Angie, Terri, Laurie, Julie, Alissa, Sarah, Sandy, Christine, Rich, Jenetah, Victoria, Jackie, Noemie, and Lindsay. I love you all!

CHAPTER SIXTY-NINE

About the author

Jacci lives with her husband in Nevada's high desert. They spend their mornings hiking through the sagebrush with their dog, Rosie.

Jacci loves chocolate, babies, and coffee with friends. She's worn many hats in her life: therapist, school counselor, campus minister, and mom. Her favorite hats are her writer and grandmother hats, which come in wild colors and don't fit too tightly.

Jacci is the author of twelve books for middle grade and young adults and three for adults.

You can find Jacci on most social media sites under her name or her website at www.jacciturner.com

Before you go I'd appreciate an honest review on Amazon or other retailers!